Designing with Conifers

Designing with Conifers

THE BEST CHOICES FOR
YEAR-ROUND INTEREST
IN YOUR GARDEN

Richard L. Bitner

Timber Press
Portland • London

Page 1: *Pinus densiflora* 'Oculus-draconis'; pages 2–3: A garden of diverse conifers; page 5: *Chamaecyparis obtusa* 'Crippsii'

The Haseltine Building
133 S.W. Second Avenue, Suite 450
Portland, Oregon 97204-3527
www.timberpress.com

2 The Quadrant
135 Salusbury Road
London NW6 6RJ
www.timberpress.co.uk

Printed in China
Interior designed by Lila Braker

Library of Congress Cataloging-in-Publication Data

Bitner, Richard L.
    Designing with conifers / Richard L. Bitner. — 1st ed.
        p. cm.
    Includes bibliographical references and index.
    ISBN 978-1-60469-193-1
    1. Conifers—Varieties. 2. Gardens—Design. I. Title.
    SB428.B552 2011
    715—dc22
                                                              2010032644

A catalog record for this book is also available from the British Library.

For my friend,
Elliot L. Heffner

Contents

ACKNOWLEDGMENTS

THANKS TO ALL the homeowners, gardeners, and garden designers who have so bigheartedly allowed me to visit and photograph their gardens, even though I should always have seen it the week before.

And a special thanks to those helpers who tend the many public botanic gardens, parks, and arboreta throughout the United States and in Canada, Germany, Scotland, and the Czech Republic where I have visited and photographed for my books and lectures. To a person they have always been willing to answer questions, guide me to yet another treasure, and recommend additional gardens.

Worthy of special mention also are the folks at Iseli Nursery in Boring, Oregon, who have allowed me access to photograph their brilliant displays.

And thanks to Tom Fischer, Linda Willms, and everyone at Timber Press for their encouragement with this, my third book exploring gardening with conifers.

INTRODUCTION

DESIGN WITH CONIFERS?

Conifers!

We may think of "selecting" a conifer to plop in the middle of the yard, perhaps. And undoubtedly the new homeowner expects some yews to be "installed" as foundation plants. But *design* with cedars and cypresses using the same exactness we would use in selecting companion plants in an herbaceous border?

Well, yes.

After all, what's not to like about conifers? We love their graceful shapes. Their evergreen leaves. Their sweeping branches. The magazine photos of ski trails through towering firs. The postcard pictures of topiaries in the estates of seventeenth-century French royalty. The tall cypresses lining gravel roads in romantic Italian movies.

But mixed in with our salvias and sambucus?

Well, yes.

This book is about using conifers as garden plants. Selecting them for their habit, or their foliage, or maybe for their winter color (who would have thought?). Selecting them as accents. Integrating them into the mixed border. And, yes, putting the right plant in the right place.

Perhaps no group of plants is so poorly used in our gardens, even though they play a multitude of roles in our landscapes from lush shade trees and useful hedges to foundation shrubs, groundcovers, and rock garden regulars. The complaint most often heard is "My plant got too big." Or, "Why did the lower branches all die?"

All too often fast-growing selections are planted too close to structures and to one another. They soon block windows and hang over driveways and the owner is forced to butcher them. We don't have to drive far to find beautiful homes whose walls and doorways are hidden by yews or arborvitaes. Plants that should have been removed years earlier are tolerated. Sometimes a gardener should be brutal.

The same plants are used repeatedly. The front side of every suburban house looks the same. Mulch and meatballs.

It's time to use conifers in more creative ways.

It's time to take advantage of their many attributes.

Opposite: The variety of shapes, sizes, and colors that conifers offer is truly staggering—and a gift to designers.

11

Without the strong presence of the background conifers, this border—rich as it is—would lose in overall effectiveness.

It's time to act.

The focus of this book is about making better choices when we select conifers for our landscapes or integrate them into our mixed borders. This will require changing our thinking about conifers. It means doing some reading and making inquiries before buying and planting conifers. They are not cheap, nor are they like rose bushes that we might move around from year to year.

This is not a how-to or step-by-step book on designing gardens. Readers will not need to get out their graph paper and straight edges. It is not about making drawings to scale with little marks indicating the required drifts of three, five, seven, or nine plants. Nor is a color wheel required. There will be no pretending to understand the differences among hues, shades, tints, or value discussed in books on color theory.

Countless books are available on garden design, though generally with emphasis on the shaping of borders and the selection of paving materials for pathways. Most serious gardeners already have a strong sense of vision in their use of plants—except in the case of conifers.

This book is meant to be an introduction to the balance conifers

provide throughout a garden. And their versatility. Whatever landscape situation or challenge exists, there is an appropriate conifer to be had for that site. With the palette that is available today a designer can find a conifer to use for virtually every design requirement.

Finally, this book is not about developing a gardening "style," although it will discuss and illustrate the ways conifers can be used in all manner of gardens.

Conifers provide structure—as well as valuable color contrast—in the fall garden.

Why Color Alone Is Not Enough

Many of us begin to garden because we've fallen in love with flowers. Most likely it's their color that has caught our eyes. Color is one of the most important aspects of a garden since we naturally respond so strongly to it. Calendar pictures always feature flowers, not spent seed capsules.

Later we begin to enjoy the contrasting forms of the blooms. Eventually we realize the importance of foliage in our plans. But all too often we still end up with little more than a plant collection.

When we sit back to view our gardens, we sense that something is missing, something more is needed if the gardens are to be gratifying. It's likely that what is missing are structure and a sense of unity. The presence of recurrent shapes or repeated lines to form a backbone that carries the display through all the seasons. That is, a strong architectural framework was not laid out first as a background for the display of color.

At the same time, we do like plants in our gardens that change through the season. A viburnum with soft pink buds that open to a white blush or the fall color of switch grass foliage. But deciduous shrubs are bare several months of the year and herbaceous plants turn into withered straw-colored blobs. Sometimes gardens that draw busloads of camera-laden visitors in summer have little to look at in winter.

The Role of Conifers

We plant conifers because most of them don't change much at all. They add structure and continuity. They provide stunning accents during the growing season and maintain balance throughout the year.

Structure is a primary component in designing a successful planting. In summer conifers blend with woody shrubs and herbaceous plants to anchor the sequence of colorful blooms that insure a picture perfect border. But once the herbaceous plants go dormant, the conifers come forward and a completely new rhythm becomes apparent.

Their advantage is their longevity, the slow pace with which they change, both of which help develop a sense of continuity. For centuries structure has been regarded as a central element in all styles and periods. Designers argue that once a strong framework is created, all sorts of much more informal planting can then take place within it.

We need to balance the big color statements with patches of calm—with the soothing green of a yew (*Taxus*) and the gray of a Korean fir (*Abies koreana*). Conifers add tranquility to a garden and give a garden life in the winter. Conifers give a sense of permanence.

Green is central to any color scheme. It offers us a sense of comfort all year long. It creates a visually restful space between other colors. But "green" hardly describes the great varieties of colors that conifers display. There is the yellow-green of a golden arborvitae (*Thuja*), the mint green of the early spring emerging foliage of bald-cypress (*Taxo-*

Conifers aren't just about shape—conifer foliage introduces many textures and subtle colors to the garden.

dium distichum), the gray-green of a Colorado spruce (*Picea pungens*), and the black-green of yews (*Taxus*).

But take note: conifers offer color that goes beyond just green. There are the blues of cedars and junipers, the gold of thread-leaved false cypress (*Chamaecyparis pisifera* 'Filifera Aurea'), and, in winter, the clear yellow of Chief Joseph lodgepole pine (*Pinus contorta* var. *latifolia* 'Chief Joseph'), and the bronze and plum of cryptomeria.

Although the textural quality of conifer needles is often the last thing on the gardener's mind, consider the pliable and rubbery foliage of Japanese umbrella-pine (*Sciadopitys verticillata*), the silver sparkle of many groundcover junipers, the knife-sharp leaves of a monkey-puzzle (*Araucaria araucana*), and the unexpected softness of the oriental spruce (*Picea orientalis*). Characteristics like these can add appeal and versatility when combined with other plants. The ideal is to link our plants together in a subtle way so they blend as if they have always been there, growing together simply and naturally.

The Many Ways to Use Conifers

Sometimes the style of the garden itself—formal or informal—holds it together, but more often a sense of unity is achieved through the repetition of the same plants, plant forms, colors, or textures throughout a garden. The use of related elements that flow through the plantings

helps create a unified whole. Integrating conifers into a border provides a backbone for the display. It is important to balance contrasting forms and repeated forms. A sense of uniformity is the quality that ties a design together.

In the smaller garden or the mixed border the slow-growing conifers provide vertical accents, mounding forms confer harmony, weeping and cascading selections move in the breeze and their foliage adds color. We can even include conifers that change color in the winter. Some conifers are so striking they are planted in a larger landscape as specimens to be admired just for themselves.

Garden design involves space—how we look at it and move around in it. It's desirable to break up our gardening space, no matter how small, so that not everything is visible at once. Different sections of the garden can have their own character. Many conifers are grown to shape them into hedges to provide backgrounds for herbaceous plantings or for screening or windbreaks. Microclimates created by screening often permit us to grow plants not normally hardy in our zone.

Opposite: Conifer hedges are ideal for creating discrete spaces, or "rooms," within a larger design.

Below: Spikes and globes in a public garden.

Conifer topiaries can be seen in large botanic gardens as well as in patio containers. Spires add lift to our plantings; they are a dominant visual element in any combination and are often effective in small groups. Spiky conifers provide relief from the mounding masses of most herbaceous plants.

Globes are rounded and clumpy conifers, sometimes flat-topped, that contrast with softer shapes. They are often less formal than vertical plants. Many slow-growing conifers keep their rounded, compact shapes and do not require pruning.

Weeping and cascading plants are more liquid as they mimic fountains or creep over walls, softening geometric forms. They are especially useful on slopes and grade changes.

It is important to move around a garden when considering where to place a large specimen tree that will be there for decades. Don't forget to check out the spot from an upper window. Visualizing a plant's spread at maturity is particularly important when planting in proximity to parking areas.

The Problem of Foundation Plantings

Foundation plantings came about during the Victorian era when huge homes sat on massive foundations and large shrubs were used to anchor the houses and bring them back into scale with their surroundings. We're so used to that approach that we still think our contemporary homes look naked without them.

In some neighborhoods foundation plantings continue to be mandatory dress code for houses, a response to the expectations of others. Why not an island planting set away from the house or borders along a winding path leading up to the entrance? Suggestions for breaking away from this blobs-in-a-row across the front of the house are discussed later in this book.

Dwarf Conifers

Foundation plantings and front yard gardens are the ideal places to utilize dwarf conifers. The world of dwarf conifers is large, rather specialized, and little explored by the average homeowner. This is unfortunate, because while dwarf conifers are often regarded as exotic, they are extremely useful plants, especially in foundation plantings and integrated into mixed borders where slow growth is one of their

Opposite, top: The contrast of shapes and the incorporation of plants other than conifers distinguish this foundation planting from the usual blobs and kettledrums.

Opposite, bottom: Conifers grown as bonsai and in troughs.

most important assets. Many of us, when we start studying and looking for these garden-sized conifers for the first time are surprised by a new array of good landscaping specimens we didn't know existed.

It is even possible to garden with conifers without a garden! There are miniature, extremely slow-growing hardy conifers that can be grown in containers and trough gardens year-round.

Conifer Collections

Just like certain collectors in the orchid crowd, there are crazed coniferites who collect conifers for the sake of collecting. They keep careful acquisition records and diligently place weather-resistant labels by each plant in the garden. Their collections have year-round interest but little else to offer except the satisfaction that comes from having every last cultivar of the common Norway spruce (*Picea abies*)

Proof that a conifer collection can have esthetic merit.

and comparing notes with other collectors at society meetings. Not unlike stamp collecting.

In contrast, other collectors combine their treasures artfully and imaginably, and open their gardens for touring groups. Some collectors have endowed and opened their collections permanently to the public for study and pleasure. The amazing Bickelhaupt Collection in Clinton, Iowa, is an example. Other renowned collectors have donated their plants to arboretums like the celebrated Gotelli Collection in the National Arboretum in Washington, DC, and the Harper Dwarf and Rare Conifer Collection at Michigan State University in Tipton, Michigan.

Specialty conifer nurseries often have permanent display gardens to show off what they are growing for sale. One such extensive exhibit is at the well-known Iseli Nursery in Boring, Oregon.

Stopping by a good local nursery provides a beginning for exploring plant possibilities. However, be aware that many of the dwarf and

Conifer display at Iseli Nursery near Portland, Oregon.

slow-growing cultivars may have to be special ordered. Visiting public gardens, many of which have extensive conifer collections, despite their scale and professional maintenance, can often suggest principles that can be adapted to home gardens. See the list of places to see conifers at the back of this book.

Cultural Notes About Conifers

A gardener always has to work with the physical limitations (and opportunities) of the site. Good design is not just about coming up with an admirable planting scheme, but responding to the site as it is and developing a relationship with it and the plants that will thrive in those conditions. New home owners may have to take a year or more to learn completely which are the wet or dry parts of the garden, which are more exposed to wind, and which get winter sun and the like.

Conifers in the Botanic Garden, Hamburg, Germany.

Identifying areas that have extreme conditions is critical when it comes to making planting plans and selecting appropriate cultivars. It is important to understand thoroughly our own garden and its year-round climatic conditions.

Generally speaking, conifers are not finicky garden plants. It is hard to generalize about their soil requirements although they will do best in well-drained, sandy or clay loam soil in full sun. Conifers prefer soil that is on the acid side. The best way to determine the kind of soil in a garden is to send samples to the local Cooperative Extension service for a pH analysis.

It is said that conifers will acidify the soil themselves because their leaves are acidic. Very alkaline soil presents a problem because it limits the availability of essential nutrients. The best choices for these soils are yew (*Taxus*) and true cedars (*Cedrus*).

Dry sandy sites are among the most difficult sites for plants and typically, along with oaks (*Quercus*), conifers such as cypress (*Cupressus*), juniper (*Juniperus*), and pine (*Pinus*) will be the most drought tolerant. Other suggestions for summer-dry areas are listed on page 281.

Clay and waterlogged soils make low levels of oxygen available to plant roots during the wet seasons but are often dry during other periods. Bald-cypress (*Taxodium distichum*) and dawn redwood (*Metasequoia glyptostroboides*) are tolerant of these conditions. Giant arborvitae (*Thuja plicata*) and eastern arborvitae (*T. occidentalis*) are other possibilities for wet spots. Most conifers will grow in clay soils but will usually take longer to be established.

Unfortunately planning gardens in newly built subdivisions is challenging because the good topsoil has been removed and all too often was replaced with only a few inches of topsoil. The clay soil just under the surface presents drainage problems. To test for drainage, dig a hole about 20 inches (50 cm) deep and fill it with water. Let it drain and refill it. If the second filling does not drain within two hours, then for most conifers it would be prudent to either amend the soil to improve the drainage or create raised beds. If a heavy soil can't be improved, there are still some choices (see "Conifers for Wet Spots"). And for tough sites, there are 10 reliable conifers that will adapt to a wide range of cultural conditions; these are readily available in fine nurseries, and are discussed and illustrated in multiple chapters in this book (see "Workhorse Conifers" for a list).

Although the majority of conifers want to grow in full sun, a few

WORKHORSE CONIFERS

- *Cedrus atlantica* (Atlas cedar)
- *Chamaecyparis obtusa* (hinoki false cypress)
- *Chamaecyparis pisifera* 'Filifera Aurea' (golden thread-leaved false cypress)
- *Cryptomeria japonica* (Japanese-cedar)
- *×Cupressocyparis leylandii* (Leyland cypress)
- *Juniperus virginiana* 'Corcorcor' (eastern red-cedar)
- *Metasequoia glyptostroboides* (dawn redwood)
- *Taxodium distichum* (bald-cypress)
- *Taxus baccata* (English yew)
- *Thuja occidentalis* 'Smaragd' (eastern arborvitae)

tolerate partial shade (see page 195), and some are suitable for regions with a long, hot growing season (see "Conifers for Southern Gardens").

Spacing is critical when designing with conifers since the plant we put in will likely take some time to reach mature height and width. It is always better to leave too much space between plants than too little, and always be aware where drain pipes empty. Keep all plants at least 4 feet (1.2 m) away from the house, often more.

Be sure conifers are planted at the level at which they were originally grown. It is important to watch plants that have been grafted and remove any growth arising from below the graft site.

It is best to pay close attention to the likely growth rate of a selection and select slow-growing cultivars for borders to avoid the need to prune. Conifers vary in their tolerance to severe pruning and the right cut can spell the difference between a plant that looks butchered and one that is pleasing to the eye.

Horticulture is growing plants well but design is arranging them well. All aspects of garden development should involve both considerations with equal enthusiasm. Of course, anything involving planting always has to make allowances for the fact that plants will never grow in ways that are entirely predictable.

Can you design your own garden?

Of course, even though you may not consider yourself a designer. What you can do is make better choices when you pick your conifers, opting for those that are appropriate for the site and doing your best to create harmonious relationships among your plants.

Gardening is a process to enjoy, learn from, and to refine continually. Making it happen in your garden is up to you. Then one day perhaps your garden will be an inspiration to others.

1

Shape

Spiky Conifers

WE NEVER FAIL TO NOTICE the vertical accents of spiky forms in gardens whether they are plants or architectural elements. No category of plant provides a more compelling punctuation point in a design than a narrow conifer.

Spires lead our eyes upwards, and they contrast the more horizontal planes of the garden. Often they serve to anchor looser plantings. They give a garden bed, particularly an island bed, a sense of permanence through all seasons.

Overleaf: A pair of gold towers (*Cupressus sempervirens* 'Swain's Gold') guides the visitor through an exuberant border.

Opposite: The term "fastigiate" refers to a tree with several parallel trunks growing closely together with the branches ascending.

Left: The term "columnar" refers to having the shape of a column: flat on the top with straight sides. However, the terms "fastigiate" and "columnar" are often used interchangeably.

Of course spires should not dominate the scene and distract from everything else. The smooth spires made by the natural form of some conifers and by trained topiary (see page 171) were made for formal gardens where they can draw the eye along a path or vista to a focal point.

Opposite, top: Irish yews (*Taxus baccata* 'Fastigiata') lead the eye to the fountain, another pair of yews, and a distant structure in a public garden.

Opposite, bottom: This group of narrow conifers adds drama near a formal pool in a private estate garden.

Left: Vertical conifers are especially effective in groups.

Serbian spruce (*Picea omorika*) provides the significant height appropriate in this public space without being wide-spreading. Note it retains its foliage to the ground.

Spiky Conifers A to Z

Many species of conifers that are not naturally columnar have a columnar or fastigiate selection. A few of these are described here. Your local nursery or garden center may carry others suitable to your region.

Calocedrus decurrens (incense-cedar): a slender tree with a spire-like top, reaches 50 ft. (15 m) tall in cultivation, very drought tolerant, beautiful cinnamon-red deeply furrowed bark, has a formal appearance in the landscape.

Calocedrus decurrens

Cephalotaxus harringtonia 'Fastigiata' (Japanese plum-yew): markedly upright, grows slowly, eventually distinctly vase-shaped, can reach 16 ft. (5 m) tall but is usually less than 10 ft. (3 m), deep green, almost black-green 1½ to 2½ in. (3.5 to 6 cm) long needles are arranged spirally around the stem and facing upward, can be difficult to place, but works well in a formal setting or at an "inside" corner of a structure.

Cephalotaxus harringtonia 'Korean Gold' (Japanese plum-yew): an upright, fastigiate form with new growth appearing yellow, then turning pale green, and green with season's end, foliage in whorls, should be protected from winter winds.

Chamaecyparis nootkatensis 'Green Arrow' (Alaska-cedar): a narrow form with branches that sweep straight downward close to the trunk, often forming a skirt at the base, carries snow loads well (see photo).

Chamaecyparis nootkatensis 'Van den Akker' (Alaska-cedar): one of the narrowest of all conifers. Striking.

Left: Cephalotaxus harringtonia 'Fastigiata'

Right: Cephalotaxus harringtonia 'Korean Gold'

Chamaecyparis nootka-tensis, possibly 'Van den Akker', explodes out of a mixed planting.

Cupressus sempervirens 'Totem' (Italian cypress): a very narrow upright columnar form of Italian cypress, deep green foliage, reaches 12 ft. (3.6 m) tall by 20 in. (50 cm) wide in 10 years.

Juniperus communis 'Arnold' (common juniper): a dense narrow columnar form of common juniper, silver-green foliage.

Juniperus communis 'Compressa' (common juniper): a slow-growing narrow upright dwarf, cone-shaped without shearing, fine-textured silvery blue-green foliage, grows 2 in. (5 cm) a year to 3 ft. (0.9 m) tall.

Juniperus communis 'Gold Cone' (common juniper): a slow-growing, narrow and columnar shrub or small tree, dense foliage, golden in summer, yellow-green in winter, protect from sun and wind.

Juniperus communis 'Sentinel' (common juniper): upright and columnar, almost pointed without shearing, blue-green foliage, reaches 5 ft. (1.5 m) tall.

Vertical cypresses (*Cupressus*) lead the visitor along an elevated path in a public garden.

Left: *Juniperus communis* 'Compressa'

Below: *Juniperus communis* 'Gold Cone'

Juniperus scopulorum 'Skyrocket' (Rocky Mountain juniper): a very narrow selection of Rocky Mountain juniper, 15 ft. (4.5 m) tall by 2 ft. (0.6 m) wide, blue-green foliage, darkens in winter, use as a vertical accent or in a formal design, male, does not age well.

Picea glauca 'Conica' (dwarf Alberta white spruce): dense and conical, becomes 3 to 4 ft. (0.9 to 1.2 m) tall by 18 in. (46 cm) wide in 10 to 15 years, put in a cool location with some shade and good air circulation, never loses its shape, many variations available.

Picea glauca 'Jean's Dilly' (white spruce): slower growing than 'Conica', even more tailored and darker green.

Picea glauca 'Pixie' (white spruce): an upright narrow cone with dark green needles, slow-growing, reaches 12 in. (30 cm) tall in 10 years.

Picea glauca 'Pixie Dust' (white spruce): dense and compact, emerging bud growth is yellow, reaches 16 in. (40 cm) tall in 10 years (see photo).

Picea glauca 'Rainbow's End' (white spruce): again, similar but has creamy yellow new growth, benefits from light shade to avoid burning.

Picea omorika 'Pendula' (Serbian spruce): central leader is upright with very vertical pendulous branches and a trailing skirt.

Picea glauca 'Pixie'

Picea omorika 'Pendula Bruns' (Serbian spruce): very narrow with pendulous side branches (see photo). Choice.

Picea pungens 'Iseli Fastigiate' (Colorado spruce): narrowly upright, blue foliage, subject to snow damage (see photo).

Pinus leucodermis 'Iseli Fastigiate' (Bosnian pine): slow-growing,

Pinus leucodermis 'Iseli Fastigiate'

conical, in 10 years reaches 15 ft. (4.5 m) tall but only 3 ft. (0.9 m) wide, useful for screening or as an accent.

Pinus mugo 'Fastigiata' (mugo pine): compact, columnar, 6 ft. (1.8 m) tall by 2 ft. (0.6 m) wide in 10 years, tolerates soils with low fertility and high pH as well as wind, drought, and heat.

Pinus nigra 'Arnold's Sentinel' (Austrian pine): an upright, narrow, and conical selection of Austrian pine, to 30 ft. (9 m) tall by 6 to 10 ft. (1.8 to 3 m) wide, excellent salt tolerance in maritime climates.

Sequoiadendron giganteum 'Pendulum' (giant sequoia): a tall pillar with branches completely pendulous and parallel with the trunk,

Sequoiadendron giganteum 'Pendulum'

sometimes leaning this way and that, with upward branches contorted, growing upright, then dipping and growing upright again, often multiple leaders.

Taxus baccata 'David' (English yew): an upright form with yellow needles.

Taxus baccata 'Fastigiata' (Irish yew): markedly upright, dense broad column, black-green needles whorled around the stem, fast-growing, can reach 30 ft. (9 m) tall, will take hard pruning and always sprouts from old wood, female.

Taxus baccata
'Fastigiata'

Left: *Taxus baccata* 'Standishii'

Right: *Taxus ×media* 'Beanpole'

Taxus baccata 'Standishii' (English yew): slow-growing dense column of tightly packed branches, golden yellow foliage, female.

Taxus ×media 'Beanpole' (hybrid yew): very narrow, only 8 in. (20 cm) wide, and dense fastigiate female, slow-growing

Taxus ×media 'Flushing' (hybrid yew): upright, narrow, columnar, glossy dark green foliage with bright red cones, reaches 12 to 15 ft. (3.6 to 4.5 m) tall but only 3 ft. (0.9 m) wide.

Thuja occidentalis 'Degroot's Spire' (eastern arborvitae): slow-growing, rich green, very nice narrow, tightly branched, upright form but requires attention to be sure it develops a central leader, bronzes slightly in winter.

Thuja occidentalis 'Smaragd' (eastern arborvitae): emerald green vertical foliage sprays, grows rapidly, reaching 15 ft. (4.5 m) tall by 4 ft. (1.2 m) wide in 15 years, stays compact, narrow and upright, unaffected by snow or ice loads if trained to a single leader, maintains color all seasons, good for hedging, heat- and cold-tolerant (see photo).

Thuja orientalis 'Golden Minaret' (oriental arborvitae): slow-growing, slender, cone-shaped, gold foliage, reaches 4 ft. (1.2 m) tall, does not tolerate wet sites.

Left: *Taxus ×media* 'Flushing'

Right: *Thuja occidentalis* 'Degroot's Spire'

Mounding and Globe-shaped Conifers

PLANTS THAT ARE ROUNDED GLOBES create bulk in our borders and give them a sense of solidity and mass. Some conifer selections have a naturally crisp mounding outline, others less so. Many gardeners feel the urge to shape plants that are mounding into strict spheres rather than let them grow into their naturally balanced habits—an urge that should probably be resisted unless the goal is to create topiary.

Rounded forms add weight and punctuation to a planting. The beauty of these forms is enhanced by juxtaposing them with spiky conifers and the looser foliage of perennials and weaving plants. They hold together all the other plantings and give a sense of permanence and weight against the flux of herbaceous plants. They are often repeated for impact or to create balance. Globes are practical for foundation plantings as there are many dwarfs that are slow-growing and require minimal maintenance, making it easier to keep the planting in scale over time.

Opposite: This compact rounded pine (*Pinus*) softens the stone hardscaping.

Below: A green spruce (*Picea*) globe accompanies the changing display of herbaceous plants.

Above: A globose Japanese-cedar (*Crypto-meria japonica*) in an Asian-style garden echoes the shape of the dogwood on the other side of the pool.

Right: A golden hiba arborvitae (*Thujopsis*) brightens up a shady spot.

Opposite, top: This soft compact arborvitae (*Thuja*) echoes the forms of the nearby rocks.

Opposite, bottom: A gray fir (*Abies*) contrasts with the fall color of the Japa-nese maple, hellebores, and the variegated yucca.

Opposite, top: A flat-topped, slow-growing Norway spruce (*Picea abies*) cultivar balances this planting.

Opposite, bottom: The looser form of the pine (*Pinus*) joins the formality of the clipped boxwood in a spring display.

Above: This pale green arborvitae (*Thuja*) balances the verticals of pearl millet (*Pennisetum glaucum* 'Purple Majesty') and feather reed grass (*Calamagrostis* 'Karl Foerster').

Left: An irregularly rounded Boulevard falsecypress (*Chamaecyparis pisifera* 'Boulevard') in a rock garden.

Right: A miniature pine (*Pinus*) in a landscape of sedums and hens and chicks.

Below: This flat-topped pine (*Pinus*) is in perfect scale with low-growing rock-garden plants.

Opposite, top: A tiny globe with rock garden plants.

Opposite, bottom: This hinoki falsecypress (*Chamaecyparis obtusa*) acts as a full stop in a colorful bed beneath a formal patio.

Naturally Rounded Medium-sized Slow-growing Conifers A to Z

Abies concolor 'Compacta' (compact concolor fir): irregularly rounded, reaching 2 ft. (0.6 m) tall after many years.

Abies concolor 'Glauca Compacta' (concolor fir): similar to 'Compacta'.

Abies koreana 'Cis' (Korean fir): bushy with rich dark green needles, growing 1 in. (2.5 m) a year (see photo).

Abies koreana 'Doni-Tajuso' (Korean fir): dark green foliage on a flat round plant, grows 1 in. (2.5 cm) a year.

Abies koreana 'Silberkugel' (Korean fir): similar to 'Doni-Tajuso' in shape, dark green needles with silver undersides, hence the name meaning "silver bullet," good for troughs and rock gardens (see photo).

Abies procera 'Blaue Hexe' (noble fir): broad, flat, spherical habit, short, powder-blue needles, hence the name meaning "blue witch," growing 1 to 2 in. (2.5 to 5 cm) a year.

Chamaecyparis lawsoniana 'Green Globe' (Lawson false cypress): dense rounded and compact, eventually reaching 1 to 2 ft. (0.3 to 0.6 m).

Chamaecyparis lawsoniana 'Pixie' (Lawson false cypress): a broadly rounded dwarf with dense blue-green foliage.

Chamaecyparis lawsoniana 'Schneeball' (Lawson false cypress): a white variegated globose dwarf, name means "snow ball."

Chamaecyparis nootkatensis 'Compacta' (Alaska-cedar): dense rounded bushy habit with light green foliage in dense flat sprays, reaches 6 ft. (1.8 m) tall.

Chamaecyparis obtusa 'Coralliformis' (hinoki false cypress): a dwarf and bushy mound with unique dark green, twisted, cordlike foliage, reaches 5 ft. (1.5 m) tall after 25 years.

Chamaecyparis obtusa 'Elmwood Gold' (hinoki false cypress): a rounded bush with bright yellow foliage in summer, bronze in winter, reaches 4 ft. (1.2 m) tall by 3 ft. (0.9 m) wide in 10 years.

Chamaecyparis obtusa 'Kosteri' (hinoki false cypress): an upright bushy form with bright green twisting, mossy foliage that bronzes in winter, eventually reaches 5 ft. (1.5 m) tall by 4 ft. (1.2 m) wide, appreciates protection from drought and harsh winds, a favorite.

Chamaecyparis pisifera 'Aurea Nana' (sawara-cypress): slow-growing globose dwarf, golden foliage.

Chamaecyparis pisifera 'Golden Mop' (sawara-cypress): low and mounding, bright golden color, fine thread foliage, slow to establish.

Chamaecyparis obtusa 'Kosteri'

Cryptomeria japonica 'Compacta' (Japanese-cedar): blue-green needles, densely branched.

Cryptomeria japonica 'Globosa' (Japanese-cedar): broadly rounded to 5 ft. (1.5 m) tall, dense blue-green foliage turning bronze-red in winter.

Cryptomeria japonica 'Globosa Nana' (Japanese-cedar): similar to 'Globosa' but smaller, mounding at 2 to 3 ft. (0.6 to 0.9 m) tall in 10 years (see photo).

Juniperus virginiana 'Globosa': rounded shrub to 5 ft. (1.5 m) tall, bright green in summer, dulls in winter.

Picea omorika 'Nana' (Serbian spruce): broad-growing shrub, short blue-green needles with silver undersides on short branches.

Picea omorika 'Pimoko' (Serbian spruce): similar to *P. omorika* 'Nana' but smaller.

Picea orientalis 'Nana' (oriental spruce): dense globose form usually not more than 3 ft. (0.9 m) tall.

Pinus mugo 'ENCI'

Pinus mugo 'ENCI' (mugo pine): selected for superior and uniform mounding habit, reaches 5 to 6 ft. (1.5 to 1.8 m) tall with equal spread, attractive spring candles are light green.

Pinus mugo 'Honeycomb' (mugo pine): squat and globe-shaped, lime green in summer changing to yellow in winter.

Pinus mugo 'Mops' (mugo pine): formal compact and globose form that reaches 3 ft. (0.9 m) tall, resinous bright green needles.

Pinus mugo 'Pot o' Gold' (mugo pine): slow-growing, mounding and compact, green foliage in summer, orange-yellow foliage in winter.

Pinus mugo 'Sherwood Compact' (mugo pine): compact and globe-shaped, remains dark green all seasons.

Pinus mugo 'Teeny' (mugo pine): very tight, dense, rounded, short-needled plant with dark green winter color.

Pinus nigra 'Helga' (Austrian pine): rounded, upright form with bright green needles and white buds.

Pinus strobus 'Blue Shag' (eastern white pine): dense, rounded habit and silver-blue needles.

Pinus strobus 'Nana' (eastern white pine): dense, spreading, irregular mound, slow-growing with puffy bunches of blue-green foliage.

Pinus strobus 'Pygmaea' (eastern white pine): a globose dwarf with bright green needles.

Left: *Pinus mugo* 'Teeny'

Below: *Pinus strobus* 'Pygmaea'

Pinus strobus 'Radiata' (eastern white pine): a great garden white pine, slow-growing and globose, to 4 ft. (1.2 m) tall after 25 years, often labeled 'Nana'.

Pinus sylvestris 'Nana' (Scots pine): slow-growing small bush with blue-gray needles.

Pinus thunbergii 'Banshosho' (Japanese black pine): dense and globose with rich green foliage.

Sequoiadendron giganteum 'Pygmaeum' (giant sequoia): dense conical dwarf with light green foliage.

Thuja occidentalis 'Boothii' (eastern arborvitae): rounded and dense, rich green foliage, becomes flat-topped with age, reaches 6 to 10 ft. (1.8 to 3 m) tall.

Thuja occidentalis 'Conica Densa' (eastern arborvitae): dense and rounded with upright branching.

Thuja occidentalis 'Globosa' (eastern arborvitae): dense and rounded, deep green foliage.

Thuja occidentalis 'Golden Globe' (eastern arborvitae): globose, wide-spreading, soft yellow foliage said not to scorch, slow-growing, reaches 4 ft. (1.2 m) tall.

Thuja occidentalis 'Hetz Midget' (eastern arborvitae): broad, rounded, dense dark green foliage turns bronze-purple in winter, extremely slow-growing, reaches 3 to 4 ft. (0.9 to 1.2 m) tall (see photo).

Thuja plicata 'Whipcord' (giant arborvitae): many-branched mounding bush with long yarnlike foliage, looks like a glossy green rag mop, bronzes in winter.

Tsuga canadensis 'Sherwood Compact' (eastern hemlock): compact globe, twisted branch structure with dark green foliage, 4 ft. (1.2 m) tall by 5 ft. (1.5 m) wide in 10 years.

Opposite, top: *Thuja occidentalis* 'Golden Globe'

Opposite, bottom: *Thuja plicata* 'Whipcord', the coolest and weirdest of all globes!

Weeping and Cascading Conifers

MATURE SPECIMENS OF WEEPING PLANTS—those whose limbs grow down, not up—foster strong emotions within gardeners. To some they represent calmness, restfulness, contemplation, and wisdom. To others they conjure up classic romantic images often seen in paintings of weeping willows with a background of boats in a lake.

Many weepers are more compact than the typical species, making them easier to use in smaller, contemporary landscapes. They add to the year-round interest in the garden with their unique growth habit which contrasts with upright plants. Others like to spread their limbs and creep around a larger space. Many are living sculptures and create a focal point for an entire garden.

Some pendulous plants originate as chance seedlings, that is, as genetic mutations. Most plants have a single growing point that re-

Opposite: A living sculpture: *Sequoiadendron giganteum* 'Pendulum'.

Below: Weeping conifers like this *Cedrus deodara* 'Silver Mist' are as valuable for their texture as for their form.

mains dominant so that the whole trunk grows straight up, but in weeping trees this control mechanism is somehow disrupted. New plants are propagated by rooting cuttings or grafting.

Quite a few weeping conifers are available to the home gardener. Their habit makes them graceful and interesting, and every specimen is unique and different. Some go predictably upright with a rigid spire while their branches hug the frames. Others are not predictable and need supports to train them where they are wanted.

Weeping and cascading conifers are divided into four groups in this chapter. In the first group are conifers with an upright pyramidal growth habit and gently weeping branches. Conifers in the second group are also upright growing, but they are strongly spikelike rather than pyramidal and their branches are sharply downward growing. A third group of weepers includes plants that do not grow upright naturally. These have to be trained to grow upright using various supports such as bamboo stakes. In the fourth group of weepers are the low-growing, groundcovering conifers.

Upright Pyramidal Growth with Weeping Lateral Branches

Conifers in this first group of weepers are reliable upright growers, forming beautiful pyramidal shapes naturally. They need no training, and their lateral branches hang downward gracefully.

Chamaecyparis nootkatensis 'Jubilee' (Alaska-cedar): more narrowly weeping than 'Pendula', and with descending branches of rich green foliage, fast-growing.

Chamaecyparis nootkatensis 'Pendula' (Alaska-cedar): an elegant weeping tree with pendulous secondary branches, two forms in cultivation, one leaner and dense, the other fuller with widely spaced sweeping branches (see photo).

Juniperus rigida 'Pendula' (needle juniper): a broad and irregular habit, down-swept branches with straight branchlets, to 20 ft. (6 m) tall, tolerates hot, dry conditions.

Juniperus scopulorum 'Tolleson's Weeping' (Rocky Mountain juniper): a broad conical tree with drooping branchlets, silver-gray foliage, reaches 20 ft. (6 m) tall, needs only 10 in. (25 cm) of water annually.

Upright Terminal Growth with Strictly Pendulous Lateral Branches

Conifers in this second group of weepers are also upright growing as in the first group, but they are strongly spikelike rather than pyramidal, and their branches grow sharply downward. The plants are pencil-thin and thus suitable for narrow spaces.

Abies alba 'Green Spiral' (European silver fir): a narrow, pendulous tree with side branches that spiral outward and down, dark green glossy needles, growing 6 to 12 in. (15 to 30 cm) a year.

Chamaecyparis lawsoniana 'Dik's Weeping' (Lawson false cypress): an open-growing green tree with pendulous branchlets, slow-growing.

Chamaecyparis nootkatensis 'Green Arrow' (Alaska-cedar): a narrow form with branches that sweep straight downward close to the trunk, often forming a skirt at the base, could be planted in groups (see photo).

Chamaecyparis nootkatensis 'Van den Akker' (Alaska-cedar): one of the narrowest forms, the leading shoot typically droops, needs plenty of moisture. Striking.

Larix kaempferi 'Stiff Weeping' (Japanese larch): similar to *L. decidua* 'Pendula' with foliage more compact and close to the trunk.

Picea glauca 'Pendula' (white spruce): formal narrow cone with weeping branches, soft blue-green foliage, grows slowly to 30 ft. (9 m) tall by 15 ft. (4.5 m) wide, does not need staking.

Picea omorika 'Pendula' (Serbian spruce): central leader is upright with very vertical pendulous branches and a trailing skirt, slower growing.

Picea omorika 'Pendula Bruns' (Serbian spruce): very narrow with strongly pendulous side branches. Stunning!

Sequoiadendron giganteum 'Pendulum' (giant sequoia): tall pillar with branches completely pendulous and parallel with trunk, sometimes leaning this way and that, with upward branches contorted, growing upright, then dipping and growing upright again, often multiple leaders (see photo). Freaky.

Nonupright Terminal Growth with Weeping Lateral Branches

A third group of weepers includes conifers that do not grow upright unless they are trained to do so. Some of them have serpentine leaders, others form nestlike bushes. Various supports, such as bamboo stakes, are needed to train these conifers to grow in a particular direction.

Among the most widely and easily grown of this type of plant is the weeping blue Atlas cedar (*Cedrus atlantica* 'Glauca Pendula'). It has broad appeal as it displays its clusters of silver-blue needles among sinewy, flexible limbs. Because of its magnetism this cultivar is frequently planted by home gardeners, because it is all too often improperly situated.

Cedrus atlantica 'Glauca Pendula' and 'Fastigiata' growing side by side in an urban public garden.

Cedrus atlantica 'Glauca Pendula' (weeping blue Atlas cedar): serpentine leader with weeping branches and steel-blue needles, needs to be supported and well positioned, once established grows 8 to 16 in.

(20 to 40 cm) a year, stunning trained to form an archway or embrace a pergola or fence. A living sculpture.

Juniperus communis 'Horstmann' (common juniper): spreading and irregular with prickly pendulous blue-green foliage, grows up to 12 in. (30 cm) a year, accepts pruning.

Larix decidua 'Puli' (European larch): weeping form used as groundcover or cascading from the highest point of staking, vivid golden yellow fall color.

Larix decidua 'Varied Directions' (European larch): wider than tall, branches go out and up from this vigorous spreading plant, then arch down and cover the ground, sometimes grafted as a high standard. Listed various ways.

Picea abies 'Pendula' (Norway spruce): vigorous weeping tree, needs to be trained on a stake to the desired height and then allowed to drape, often has unusual shapes, if not staked will be 20 ft. (6 m) wide and only 4 ft. (1.2 m) tall, a collective name, often called 'Inversa'.

A pendulous *Larix* tumbling over a wall.

Above, left: A young *Picea abies* 'Pendula' in an island bed.

Above, right: *Picea abies* 'Inversa' growing with *Nepeta* 'Walker's Low'.

Opposite, top: *Pinus strobus* 'Pendula' high pruned in a Japanese-style garden.

Opposite, bottom: *Pseudotsuga menziesii* 'Pendula'

Picea abies 'Reflexa' (Norway spruce): similar to *P. abies* 'Pendula' in growth habit.

Picea pungens 'Glauca Pendula' (Colorado spruce): will spread along the ground or drape if trained as a standard to desired height, irregular form, very sculptural, sometimes difficult to place.

Pinus strobus 'Pendula' (eastern white pine): often multistemmed and irregular in form, the branches are horizontal with the branchlets pendulous, reaches 10 ft. (3 m) tall and wide, can be a living sculpture with its large clusters of long, twisting, graceful blue-green needles. Old specimens are wonders to behold.

Pseudotsuga menziesii 'Graceful Grace' (Douglas-fir): fast-growing with long blue-green needles, irregular upright leader, lateral branches drooping, does not need staking.

Pseudotsuga menziesii 'Pendula' (Douglas-fir): slow-growing, crown pendulous and irregular.

Tsuga canadensis 'Jeddeloh' (eastern hemlock): low-spreading bush, nestlike form with pendulous branch tips, medium green foliage, reaches 4 to 5 ft. (1.2 to 1.5 m) tall.

Above: *Tsuga canadensis* 'Pendula in a rock garden.

Opposite, top: *Cedrus deodara* 'Devinely Blue'

Opposite, bottom: *Cedrus deodara* 'Feelin' Blue'

Tsuga canadensis 'Pendula' (eastern hemlock, Sargent's hemlock): overlapping, pendulous branches, a magnificent spreading lawn specimen after several decades.

Groundcovering and Cascading
In contrast to the other groups of weepers, this fourth group consists of ground-covering conifers.

Cedrus deodara 'Devinely Blue' (deodar cedar): wide-spreading, flat-topped mound with pale gray-green new growth, drooping branch tips.

Cedrus deodara 'Feelin' Blue' (deodar cedar): dwarf spreading form with gray-blue foliage, reaches 1 ft. (0.3 m) tall by 3 ft. (0.9 m) wide in 10 years.

Cedrus deodara 'Prostrate Beauty' (deodar cedar): slow-growing spreader, soft and light textured, striking blue color, eventually forms a leader (see photo).

Cedrus deodara 'Raywood's Prostrate Dwarf' (deodar cedar): vigorous groundcover with blue needles.

Cedrus deodara 'Silver Mist' (deodar cedar): dense, conical habit with slightly drooping branches, and soft, whitish needles that are resistant to burning even in full sun, grows 6 in. (15 cm) a year (see photo)

Cedrus deo. 'Divinely...'

Cedrus deod. 'Feelin Blue'

Tsuga canadensis 'Cole'

Cephalotaxus harringtonia 'Prostrata' (Japanese plum-yew): low-growing with spreading branches, 2 to 3 ft. (0.6 to 0.9 m) tall and wide, deep dark green needles, takes shade (see photo).

Chamaecyparis pisifera 'Filifera' (sawara-cypress): dense and broadly pyramidal, finely textured stringlike sprays of green foliage draped on whiplike pendulous branches, reaches 6 to 8 ft. (1.8 to 2.5 m) tall and up to 15 ft. (4.5 m) wide, easy to grow, adds a delicate look to a border.

Chamaecyparis pisifera 'Filifera Aurea' (golden thread-leaved false cypress): like 'Filifera' but with golden yellow foliage year-round if not shaded, shape and size can be controlled by pruning, a great contrast in the winter landscape (see photo). Many similar named cultivars.

Juniperus procumbens 'Nana' (garden juniper): popular and available, forms a layered mat 1 ft. (0.3 m) tall and up to 8 ft. (2.5 m) wide, prickly, pale green foliage all seasons.

Larix decidua 'Pendula' (European larch): fast-growing, variable from wide-spreading to narrow, needs staking or could be used as a groundcover, mixed in the trade with *L. kaempferi* 'Pendula'.

Below: *Chamaecyparis pisifera* 'Filifera'

Opposite, top: *Juniperus procumbens* 'Nana' cascading over a stone wall.

Opposite, bottom: *Larix kaempferi* 'Pendula'

Microbiota decussata (Siberian cypress): cold hardy, prostrate, fine-textured, lacy leaves in flat sprays that arch over with drooping tips, needs good drainage, tolerates high shade, 12 in. (30 cm) high but spreads to 6 to 12 ft.(1.6 to 3.6 m) wide, bronzes in winter (see photo).

Pinus densiflora 'Pendula' (Japanese red pine): a weeping form, needs to be staked over a standard to display its pendulous character, can be grown as a groundcover, and is very effective planted at the top of a wall, down which its branches can cascade.

Microbiota decussata growing on a shady slope.

Pinus densiflora 'Pendula'

Taxodium distichum 'Cascade Falls' (bald-cypress): pendulous large shrub not exceeding 20 ft. (6 m) tall, deciduous sage-green foliage, red-brown bark, russet fall color.

Tsuga canadensis 'Cole's Prostrate' (eastern hemlock): slow-growing, mat-forming with branches extending flat along the ground, silver-gray center branches become exposed with maturity, useful for shady rock garden or vest-pocket garden, grows 3 ft. (0.9 m) tall in 20 years.

Taxodium distichum 'Cascade Falls'

Tsuga canadensis 'Cole's Prostrate'

2
Color

Gold Conifers

WE DO NOT USUALLY PLANT an entire garden of gold conifers. More commonly, yellow-gold plants are placed here and there as focal points to lift our spirits, add contrast to adjacent combinations, or draw our eye against the surrounding greens. The luminous quality of soft golden foliage makes shady corners less dark and stands out on overcast days. It is a warm color that can be bright and cheerful as well as somber and traditional. Both gold and greenish yellow foliage make pale lavenders, mauves, and blues look richer; oranges, pinks, and even reds blend nicely also. And, of course, green.

Gold conifers are often mixed with gray plants, though that is not pleasing to everyone's eye. They display their value most conspicuously

Overleaf: A nice example of a mixed screen.

Opposite: The gold border at PepsiCo corporate headquarters in New York. Although using gold conifers en masse is risky, it can occasionally produce dramatic results.

Below: A gold conifer—in this case a mature cultivar of *Chamaecyparis obtusa*—will always draw the eye, here in a large border.

in winter, when they give pick-up to the universal drabness of the landscape. Generally speaking, gold-foliaged conifers benefit from protection from harsh winds and strong afternoon sun since some are
scorch-prone.

Many variations of "gold" are included in the listing: creamy yellow, lemon yellow, wheat, mustard yellow, golden yellow, school bus
yellow, amber, old gold, and golden brown. Gold-foliaged conifers are
a source of bright color throughout the year and are indispensible in
the winter garden.

The pyramidal golden
Chamaecyparis obtusa
'Crippsii' in a home
border.

A landscape-sized oriental spruce cultivar (*Picea orientalis* 'Skylands').

Above: A garden juniper (*Juniperus horizontalis* 'Mother Lode') makes a golden groundcover only 2 inches (5 cm) high.

Opposite, top: *Abies nordmanniana* 'Golden Spreader'

Opposite, bottom: Foliage of *Calocedrus decurrens* 'Berrima Gold'

In addition to the popular and readily available Crippsii hinoki cypress (*Chamaecyparis obtusa* 'Crippsii'), there is no lack of gold-foliaged conifers of all sizes. From large spruces to groundcovering junipers, gold conifers brighten landscapes. And the time of gold display varies: Aureospicata oriental spruce (*Picea orientalis* 'Aureospicata') has gold new spring growth but turns green later in the season, while the deciduous maidenhair tree (*Ginkgo biloba*) turns a clear brilliant gold in the fall, and Chief Joseph lodgepole pine (*Pinus contorta* var. *latifolia* 'Chief Joseph') becomes radiant gold in midwinter.

Choice Gold Conifer Cultivars A to Z

Abies koreana 'Goldener Traum' (Korean fir): dwarf and low spreading with golden foliage in winter, name means "golden dream."

Abies nordmanniana 'Golden Spreader' (Nordmann fir): slow-growing, flat, round, and spreading habit, bright golden-yellow foliage in winter, grows 3 in. (7.5 cm) a year, leaders should be cut out. Choice.

Calocedrus decurrens 'Aureovariegata' (incense-cedar): slow-growing, columnar, variegated leaves splashed with yellow and green (see photo).

Calocedrus decurrens 'Berrima Gold' (incense-cedar): slow-growing, bright gold foliage that looks deep gold to orange in the winter, popular in winter.

Cedrus atlantica 'Aurea' (golden Atlas cedar): conical, short golden-yellow needles in first year's growth, reaches 25 ft. (8 m) tall.

Cedrus atlantica 'Aurea Robusta' (Atlas cedar): upright and broadly conical, branches with golden tips, more vigorous than *C. atlantica* 'Aurea', reaches 30 to 60 ft. (9 to 18 m) tall.

Cedrus deodara 'Aurea' (golden deodar cedar): fast-growing, golden-yellow needles in spring turn yellow-green, best color in full sun.

Cedrus deodara 'Gold Cascade' (deodar cedar): a slow-growing, compact weeper.

Right: *Cedrus deodara* 'Gold Cascade'

Opposite: *Cedrus deodara* 'Roman Gold'

Cedrus deodara 'Golden Horizon' (deodar cedar): semiprostrate and flat-topped with gracefully weeping branches, spreads 2 to 4 ft. (0.6 to 1.2 m) wide, golden foliage in full sun.

Cedrus deodara 'Harvest Gold' (deodar cedar): more intense yellow color than *C. deodara* 'Aurea'.

Cedrus deodara 'Roman Gold' (deodar cedar): broad irregular cone, dense bright golden-yellow foliage.

Cephalotaxus harringtonia 'Korean Gold' (Japanese plum-yew): upright form with new growth appearing yellow, then turning pale green, and green with season's end, foliage in whorls, should be protected from winter winds (see photo).

Chamaecyparis lawsoniana 'Minima Aurea' (Lawson false cypress): a broad cone with soft golden-yellow foliage, reaches 2 to 3 ft. (0.6 to 0.9 m) tall, needs winter protection.

Chamaecyparis nootkatensis 'Aurea' (golden Alaska-cedar): pyramidal, slow-growing and dense, new foliage yellow, later becoming more yellow-green.

Chamaecyparis obtusa 'Crippsii' (hinoki false cypress): slow-growing, wide-spreading branches with drooping tips, golden yellow, ferny frond foliage with good winter color, broadly conical to 15 ft. (4.5 m) tall by 18 ft. (2.5 m) wide (see photo). A choice accent plant.

Chamaecyparis obtusa 'Elmwood Gold' (hinoki false cypress): bright yellow foliage in summer, bronze in winter, reaches 4 ft. (1.2 m) tall by 3 ft. (0.9 m) wide in 10 years.

Chamaecyparis obtusa 'Fernspray Gold' (hinoki false cypress): slender and slow-growing, reaches 10 ft. (3 m) tall after many years, bright yellow foliage all year, use as an accent or can be sheared, benefits from wind protection.

Chamaecyparis obtusa 'Lemon Twist' (hinoki false cypress): threadlike, flattened, and twisted foliage with yellow highlights.

Chamaecyparis obtusa 'Meroke Twin' (hinoki false cypress): pillar-shaped dwarf with bright lemon-yellow foliage that turns deep gold, reaches 3 to 6 ft. (0.9 to 1.8 m) tall.

Chamaecyparis obtusa 'Nana Aurea' (hinoki false cypress): bright yellow cupped sprays of foliage, reaches 6 ft. (1.8 m) tall by 3 ft. (0.9 m) wide.

Chamaecyparis obtusa 'Nana Lutea' (hinoki false cypress): a compact shrub with golden cupped foliage in sun.

Chamaecyparis pisifera 'Aureovariegata' (sawara-cypress): dwarf with mottled golden yellow foliage.

Chamaecyparis pisifera 'Filifera Aurea' (golden thread-leaved false cypress): finely textured stringlike sprays of golden-yellow foliage draped on whiplike pendulous branches, colored maintained year-round if not shaded, shape and size can be controlled by pruning, a great contrast in the winter landscape. Widely available and useful in every garden design.

Chamaecyparis nootka-tensis 'Aurea'

Paired here with a pink-flowered rhododendron, golden thread-leaved false cypress (*Chamaecyparis pisifera* 'Filifera Aurea') is equally effective with a wide range of other colors.

Chamaecyparis pisifera 'Filifera Aurea Nana' (golden thread-leaved false cypress): slow-growing dwarf, eventually reverts to full size.

Chamaecyparis pisifera 'Golden Mop' (sawara-cypress): dwarf, low and mounding, bright golden color, fine thread foliage, slow to establish, protect from harsh sun.

Chamaecyparis pisifera 'Gold Spangle' (sawara-cypress): bright yellow, threadlike foliage with some sections more congested, broadly pyramidal habit, fast-growing to 7 ft. (2 m) tall by 3 ft. (0.9 m) wide, protect from harsh sun.

Chamaecyparis pisifera 'Lemon Thread' (sawara-cypress): fine-textured rich gold foliage, fast-growing to 20 ft. (6 m) tall and wide.

Chamaecyparis pisifera 'Plumosa Aurea' (sawara-cypress): fine-textured, soft golden-yellow new growth, color persists through summer, grows slowly to 30 ft. (9 m) tall.

Chamaecyparis pisifera 'Sungold' (sawara-cypress): dwarf and mounding, threadleaf foliage with gold new growth, turning green in winter, vigorous, does not need protection from sun.

Cryptomeria japonica 'Sekkan-sugi' (Japanese-cedar): dense, upright to 30 ft. (9 m) tall, foliage tipped cream to bright yellow-gold

Cryptomeria japonica
'Sekkan-sugi'

in summer, less in winter, needs protection from drying winds and full sun.

×*Cupressocyparis leylandii* 'Golconda' (Leyland cypress): fine-textured lemon-yellow foliage throughout the compact tree, burns in winter, reaches 20 ft. (6 m) tall.

×*Cupressocyparis leylandii* 'Gold Rider' (Leyland cypress): fast-growing with a narrow crown to 70 ft. (21 m) tall by 12 ft. (3.6 m) wide, golden foliage not burned by sun.

Cupressus arizonica 'Golden Pyramid' (Arizona cypress): gold-tinted foliage, strong grower, 15 ft. (4.5 m) tall by 5 ft. (1.5 m) wide in 15 years.

Ginkgo biloba 'Autumn Gold' (maidenhair tree): upright branching, excellent autumn color, reaches 50 ft. (15 m) tall by 30 ft. (9 m) wide, male.

Ginkgo biloba 'Beijing Gold' (maidenhair tree): yellow spring growth, outstanding fall color, reaches 50 ft. (15 m) tall.

Ginkgo biloba 'Chase Manhattan' (maidenhair tree): very slow-

Cupressus arizonica
'Golden Pyramid'

Ginkgo biloba 'Variegata' foliage

growing with smaller leaves than the species, striking yellow fall color, ideal for bonsai and rock gardens.

Ginkgo biloba 'Chi-chi' (maidenhair tree): dwarf, dense, multi-stemmed habit, reaches 4 ft. (1.2 m) tall in 10 years, male.

Ginkgo biloba 'Princeton Sentry' (maidenhair tree): columnar fastigiate form, male.

Ginkgo biloba 'Variegata' (maidenhair tree): variegated green and gold, not robust, often reverts, female.

Juniperus chinensis 'Aurea' (Chinese juniper): golden columnar form, dense and narrow, mixture of prickly juvenile and smooth adult foliage, bright all seasons, protect from wind and harsh summer sun, reaches 15 ft. (4.5 m) tall, male.

Juniperus chinensis 'Daub's Frosted' (Chinese juniper): low-growing groundcover, two-toned foliage blue-green frosted with gold, quickly reaches 15 in. (38 cm) tall by 5 ft. (1.5 m) wide.

Juniperus chinensis 'Golden Glow' (Chinese juniper): low-growing with bright gold foliage, 3 ft. (0.9 m) tall by 4 ft. (1.2 m). wide

Juniperus chinensis 'Gold Lace' (Chinese juniper): vigorous and spreading with soft feathery bright gold foliage, reaches 2 ft. (0.6 m) tall by 4 ft. (1.2 m) wide.

Juniperus chinensis 'Gold Sovereign' (Chinese juniper): compact and slow-growing with bright yellow foliage all seasons, reaches up to 20 ft. (96 m) tall with a wider spread.

Above: *Juniperus chinensis* 'Saybrook Gold'

Opposite: *Metasequoia glyptostroboides* 'Ogon'

Juniperus chinensis 'Gold Star' (Chinese juniper): compact with prickly golden yellow foliage in full sun, reaches 4 ft. (1.2 m) tall by 6 ft. (1.8 m) wide.

Juniperus chinensis 'Saybrook Gold' (Chinese juniper): low and wide-spreading with center depression, horizontal branches arch slightly and droop at tips, persistent soft bright yellow juvenile foliage, doesn't always age well, 30 in. (75 cm) tall by 6 ft. (1.8 m) wide.

Juniperus communis 'Depressa Aurea' (common juniper): yellow spring foliage fades to green, vigorous and tough, broad-spreading to 4 ft. (1.2 m) tall.

Juniperus conferta 'Sunsplash' (shore juniper): prostrate groundcover, blue-green foliage with bright yellow patches in all seasons, 5 ft. (1.5 m) wide in three years.

Juniperus davurica 'Expansa Aureospicata' (daurian juniper): prickly foliage with butter-yellow variegation.

Juniperus horizontalis 'Golden Carpet' (prostrate juniper): prostrate with greenish yellow foliage.

Juniperus horizontalis 'Mother Lode' (prostrate juniper): brilliant gold in summer turning to shades of deep gold and salmon-orange with green overtones in winter, provide full sun with good drainage, very slow-growing (see photo). Choice.

Juniperus ×*pfitzeriana* 'Gold Coast' (Pfitzer juniper): fast-growing, semi-prostrate, flat-topped, and wide-spreading, bright yellow adult foliage holds color in winter.

Metasequoia glyptostroboides 'Ogon' (dawn redwood): vigorous but

slower-growing with bright gold-yellow foliage, needs some protection from scorching summer sun, deciduous.

Picea abies 'Gold Drift' (Norway spruce): yellow foliage that burns in full sun, weeping form, can be staked to desired height.

Picea abies 'Repens Gold' (Norway spruce): slow-growing, flat-topped, center builds up in time, gold foliage.

Picea glauca 'Pixie Dust' (white spruce): dense and compact, emerging bud growth is yellow, reaches 16 in. (40 cm) tall in 10 years (see photo).

Picea glauca 'Rainbow's End' (white spruce): has creamy yellow new growth, benefits from light shade to avoid burning, eventually reaches 3 to 4 ft. (0.9 to 1.2 m) tall.

Picea orientalis 'Aureospicata' (oriental spruce): new growth emerges butter-yellow in spring and is eye-catching for about six weeks above the previous year's waxy rich dark green foliage, beautifully shaped pyramidal tree can reach 60 ft. (18 m) tall by 20 ft. (6 m) wide (see photo).

Picea orientalis 'Skylands' (oriental spruce): grows slowly for several years, then 12 to 18 in. (30 to 46 cm) a year, tall and conical, foliage bright yellow year-round with dark green inner needles, give midday summer shade protection (see photo). Elegant.

Picea orientalis 'Tom Thumb' (oriental spruce): dwarf and globose with golden new foliage.

Picea pungens 'Aurea' (Colorado spruce): golden new growth, changing to blue-green in summer.

Pinus contorta var. *latifolia* 'Chief Joseph' (lodgepole pine): very slow-growing, compact, bright golden-yellow foliage.

Pinus densiflora 'Oculus-draconis' (Japanese red pine): needles marked with two yellow bands, reaches 15 ft. (4.5 m) tall by 25 ft. (8 m) wide.

Pinus mugo 'Aurea' (mugo pine): light green needles that turn bright gold in a sunny winter, a semi-dwarf, usually about 3 ft. (0.9 m) tall and wide, but sometimes up to 8 ft. (2.5 m) tall, very hardy.

Pinus mugo 'Honeycomb' (mugo pine): squat and globe-shaped, lime-green needles in summer changing to yellow in winter.

Pinus mugo 'Winter Gold' (mugo pine): an open shrub with light green twisted needles that turn bright yellow in cold weather, reaches 3 to 5 ft (0.9 to 1.5 m) tall in 10 years.

Pinus parviflora 'Ogon Janome' (golden bull's-eye pine): a form of

Pinus densiflora
'Oculus-draconis'

Pinus mugo 'Aurea'

Pinus parviflora 'Ogon Janome'

Japanese white pine with distinctive bright golden-yellow bands on green needles.

Pinus strobus 'Hillside Winter Gold' (eastern white pine): a vigorous large tree 50 to 80 ft. (15 to 24 m) tall and 20 to 40 ft. (6 to 12 m) wide, needles are blue-green in summer turning bright golden in winter.

Pinus strobus 'Louie' (eastern white pine): golden needles all seasons.

Pinus sylvestris 'Aurea' (Scots pine): foliage that turns golden yellow in early winter and is blue-green with a hint of yellow during the warm seasons, growing slowly to 30 to 50 ft. (9 to 15 m).

Pinus sylvestris 'Gold Coin' (Scots pine): slow-growing, good yellow foliage in winter.

Pinus thunbergii 'Oculus-draconis' (dragon-eyed Japanese black pine): irregularly shaped form with yellow-white stripes on its needles, most apparent in the fall.

Pinus thunbergii 'Shirome Janome' (Japanese black pine): two bright yellow bands on the needles.

Sciadopitys verticillata 'Ossorio Gold' (Japanese umbrella-pine): upright cone, golden-yellow needles, 4 ft. (1.2 m) tall by 3 ft. (0.9 m) wide in 10 years, rare and prized.

Taxus baccata 'Adpressa Aurea' (English yew): wide-spreading and dense, small yellow leaves are more golden in spring growth, brightest when grown in sun, eventually reaches 5 ft. (1.5 m) tall, female.

Taxus baccata 'David' (English yew): upright form with yellow needles.

Above: *Pinus strobus* 'Louie'

Left: *Sciadopitys verticillata* 'Ossorio Gold'

Taxus baccata 'Standishii' (English yew): slow-growing dense column of tightly packed branches, golden-yellow foliage, female.

Taxus cuspidata 'Aurescens' (Japanese yew): low-growing, compact, can be wide-spreading, small needles with yellow new growth, shade-tolerant, seldom exceeds 3 ft. (0.9 m) tall and wide, avoid wet sites.

Thuja occidentalis 'Aurea' (eastern arborvitae): globose, golden yellow foliage, does not require shearing, reaches 30 in. (75 cm) tall and wide.

Taxus baccata 'Standishii'

Thuja occidentalis 'Aureovariegata' (eastern arborvitae): good variegation, tolerates wet soil and some shade, reaches 10 to 20 ft. (3 to 6 m) tall.

Thuja occidentalis 'Cloth of Gold' (eastern arborvitae): slow-growing, round becoming conical, golden-yellow leaves during warm season, reaches 12 ft. (3.6 m) tall in 40 years.

Thuja occidentalis 'Golden Globe' (eastern arborvitae): slow-growing, globose, wide-spreading, soft yellow foliage, said not to scorch, reaches 4 ft. (1.2 m) tall (see photo).

Thuja occidentalis 'Aurea'

Thuja occidentalis 'Golden Tuffet'

Thuja occidentalis 'Golden Tuffet' (eastern arborvitae): pillow-shaped, golden-orange foliage looks braided.

Thuja occidentalis 'Lutea' (eastern arborvitae): a narrow cone, golden-yellow foliage with green interior, reaches 30 ft. (9 m) tall.

Thuja occidentalis 'Lutea Nana' (eastern arborvitae): a dwarf form of *T. occidentalis* 'Lutea'.

Thuja occidentalis 'Rheingold' (eastern arborvitae): slow-growing, oval or cone-shaped, golden-yellow foliage in summer turning deep coppery gold in winter, soft juvenile foliage, can be sheared, can reach 10 ft. (3 m) tall but usually only 2 ft. (0.6 m), will split open with snow, various forms sold under this name.

Thuja occidentalis 'Sunkist' (eastern arborvitae): dense, small, slow-growing, round-topped cone, gold-yellow color in summer, burnished gold in winter, 5 to 8 ft. (1.5 to 2.5 m) tall.

Thuja orientalis 'Aurea' (oriental arborvitae): golden foliage, various forms exist including 'Aurea Densa' and Aurea Nana'.

Thuja plicata 'Canadian Gold' (giant arborvitae): pyramidal, dense yellow foliage all seasons, reaches 65 ft. (19.5 m) tall by 20 ft. (6 m) wide.

Thuja plicata 'Stoneham Gold' (giant arborvitae): slow-growing, broad upright conical form, green in center, new growth is a bright yellow in full sun, reaches 6 ft. (1.8 m) tall by 2 ft. (8 m) wide in 15 years, popular in England. 'Collyer's Gold' is similar but brighter.

Thuja plicata 'Sunshine' (giant arborvitae): similar to *T. plicata* 'Stoneham Gold'.

Thujopsis dolabrata 'Aurea' (hiba arborvitae): yellow-gold foliage, shade tolerant, prized for distinctive white "hatchet" markings on underside of foliage.

Tsuga canadensis 'Aurea' (eastern hemlock): pyramidal, young foliage golden yellow, can be sheared.

Tsuga canadensis 'Everitt's Golden' (eastern hemlock): slow-growing stiff small tree with ascending branches, tight needles, golden yellow early in season, needs afternoon shade.

Thuja plicata 'Stoneham Gold'

Gray, Gray-Blue, and Silver Conifers

GARDENERS WITH SIZABLE PERENNIAL BORDERS love gray-foliaged plants. This is very understandable because gray foliage in a garden ties everything together and harmonizes the colors of flowers that otherwise would be jarring near one another.

Gray-foliaged plants are very effective with cool-tinted flowers: blue, lavender, mauve, and pale yellows and pinks. They often give stronger value to colors that don't have as much impact against a green background. But they also look good with, and can soften, hot colors like red, brilliant yellow, and orange. Moreover, gray looks attractive even in the harsh glare of noonday sun. Gray foliage is essential in "moon" or white gardens. As a bonus, gray plants tend to be drought tolerant (many selections of gray-leaved conifers originate from areas with low annual rainfall) and unfussy about soil conditions provided there is good drainage.

Gray- and blue-appearing conifers have the further advantage of year-long presence in the border. Although "gray" in conifers is, in actuality, a wide gradation of colors from merely bluish green to smoky blue to a silvery blue. Some will show only gray-blue new growth; many will display subtle variations as the seasons change and, definitely, with different angles of the sun.

The perception of silver and blue coloration on conifers is caused by the deposition of waxes or resins on the leaves. These waxes, which are in some cases a protective response to drought, are usually more abundant on the lower leaf surface. Additionally, there is also a wide variation in texture from the soft blue of Boulevard false cypress (*Chamaecyparis pisifera* 'Boulevard') to the very unfriendly-to-the-touch foliage of a Colorado spruce (*Picea pungens*).

Gray conifers can shine on their own as well! They make our gardens more engaging in the ebbing light of summer evenings, often the only time of day that gardeners take time to stand up from their chores and enjoy the garden.

The first conifers that come to mind when one thinks of gray are the cultivars of the native Colorado spruce, especially the cultivar 'Glauca'. However, there are dozens of selections of gray and blue-gray

Opposite: This Montgomery spruce (*Picea pungens* 'Montgomery') keeps the diverse flower colors in this border from engaging in open warfare.

Right: Some conifers like this Douglas-fir (*Pseudotsuga menziesii*) display gray only on new spring growth.

Below: Without the dwarf blue alpine fir (*Abies lasiocarpa* var. *arizonica* 'Compacta'), this combination of plants would verge on stridency.

Above: Gray conifers like this Atlas cedar cultivar (*Cedrus atlantica* 'Glauca') at Chanticleer make deservedly popular companions for cool-colored flowers like this *Clematis* 'General Sikorski'.

Left: Some conifer cones, like those of *Abies balsamea* 'Tyler Blue', are blue-gray.

conifers varying in size from those that can be used in patio containers to large landscape specimens.

The Best Gray, Blue-Gray, and Silver Conifers

Abies concolor 'Blue Cloak' (concolor fir): a weeping form, grows to 30 ft. (9 m) tall by 15 ft. (4.5 m) wide in 30 years and retains its lower branches.

Abies concolor 'Candicans' (concolor fir): one of the bluest forms, fast-growing, upright and conical, reaching 40 ft. (12 m) tall.

Abies concolor 'Candicans'

Abies concolor 'Wattezii Prostrate' (concolor fir): prostrate and spreading with pale gray-blue needles.

Abies koreana 'Blauer Eskimo' (Korean fir): a low-spreading dwarf with gray-blue needles, grows 1 in. (2.5 cm) a year.

Abies koreana 'Silberlocke' (Korean fir): tightly curved-in foliage displays silver undersides, becomes denser with age, erect violet-purple cones in spring at an early age, slow-growing. Choice.

Abies koreana 'Silberperl' (Korean fir): a congested dwarf growing 1 to 2 in. (2.5 to 5 cm) a year, much wider than tall, short needles with

Left: *Abies concolor* 'Wattezii Prostrate'

Right: *Abies koreana* 'Silberlocke' foliage.

silver undersides and buds that look like silver pearls in fall and winter. Choice.

Abies lasiocarpa var. *arizonica* 'Compacta' (dwarf blue alpine fir): densely pyramidal, densely packed soft gray-blue silvery foliage, reaches 4 ft. (1.2 m) tall by 2 ft. (0.6 m) wide after many years, drought tolerant (see photo).

Abies pinsapo 'Glauca' (Spanish fir): distinctive short, rigid, frosty blue, waxy needles that whorl around the stem, reaches 15 ft. (4.5 m) tall in 15 years and eventually 60 ft. (18 m), makes a distinctive focal point in the garden.

Abies pinsapo 'Horstmann' (Spanish fir): an attractive low-spreading compact dwarf with stiff blue foliage, useful for trough planting, grows 4 in. (10 cm) a year.

Abies procera 'Glauca' (noble fir): for the larger landscape, eye-catching blue needles, produces loads of cones.

Cedrus atlantica 'Glauca' (Atlas cedar) commonly planted selection with powdery blue needles, reaches 8 to 10 ft. (2.5 to 3 m) tall in 10 years, matures at 60 ft. (18 m) tall by 40 ft. (12 m) wide, many clones in cultivation (see photo)

Cedrus atlantica 'Glauca Pendula' (weeping blue Atlas cedar): serpentine leader with weeping branches and steel-blue needles, needs to be supported and well positioned, once established grows 8 to 16 in. (20 to 40 cm) a year, stunning trained to form an archway or embrace a pergola or fence. A living sculpture (see photo).

Cedrus deodara 'Devinely Blue' (deodar cedar): wide-spreading, flat-topped mound with pale gray-green new growth, drooping branch tips (see photo).

Cedrus deodara 'Feelin' Blue' (deodar cedar): dwarf spreading form with gray-blue foliage, reaches 1 ft. (0.3 m) tall by 3 ft. (0.9 m) wide in 10 years (see photo).

Cedrus deodara 'Karl Fuchs' (deodar cedar): more cold hardy and narrower than the species, very blue.

Cedrus deodara 'Kashmir' (deodar cedar): hardy, foliage silver-blue-green.

Cedrus deodara 'Prostrate Beauty' (deodar cedar): slow-growing spreader, soft and light textured, striking blue color, eventually forms a leader.

Cedrus deodara 'Pygmy' (deodar cedar): extremely slow-growing dwarf, less than ⅔ in. (1.7 cm) a year, useful for trough garden, blue-green needles ½ in. (1.2 cm) long.

Opposite, top: *Cedrus deodara* 'Karl Fuchs' foliage

Opposite, bottom: *Cedrus deodara* 'Prostrate Beauty'

Cedrus deodara 'Raywood's Prostrate Dwarf' (deodar cedar): a vigorous groundcover with blue needles.

Chamaecyparis lawsoniana 'Columnaris Glauca' (Lawson false cypress): narrow column 15 to 20 ft. (4.5 to 6 m) high with blue foliage in dense flat sprays, good for an accent or hedging.

Chamaecyparis lawsoniana 'Oregon Blue' (Lawson false cypress): a broad column with outstanding silver-blue foliage, drooping branch tips, grows fast, reaching 50 ft. (15 m) tall.

Chamaecyparis lawsoniana 'Pelt's Blue' (Lawson false cypress): narrow column with intense blue foliage.

Chamaecyparis lawsoniana 'Pembury Blue' (Lawson false cypress): perhaps the best bright silver-blue foliage, held in upright vertical sprays, columnar habit, 25 to 50 ft. (8 to 15 m) tall.

Left: *Chamaecyparis lawsoniana* 'Pelt's Blue'

Right: *Chamaecyparis lawsoniana* 'Pembury Blue'

Chamaecyparis pisifera 'Boulevard' (Boulevard false cypress): dense conical habit, soft silver-blue juvenile foliage becomes purple-tinged in winter, usually develops patches of dead foliage which must be pruned out, does not look good unless sheared into a bun or poodled, useful in containers, withstands heavy pruning.

Chamaecyparis pisifera 'Curly Tops' (sawara-cypress): similar to 'Boulevard' but lateral shoots have a twisted and curled appearance, juvenile leaves are glaucous blue with white bands, persistent interior brown needles, rounded habit, reaches 6 ft. (1.8 m) tall.

Chamaecyparis thyoides 'Glauca' (Atlantic white-cedar, swamp-cedar): slow-growing compact and conical shrub with silver-blue foliage, reliable.

Cunninghamia lanceolata 'Glauca' (China-fir): a landscape tree with

Left: *Chamaecyparis pisifera* 'Boulevard' poodled

Right: *Cunninghamia lanceolata* 'Glauca'

Above: ×*Cupressocyparis leylandii* 'Naylor's Blue' foliage.

Opposite, left: *Cupressus arizonica* 'Blue Ice'

Opposite, right: *Cupressus arizonica* 'Blue Pyramid'

silvery blue new foliage and pendulous habit, hardier than the species, very attractive when well grown.

×*Cupressocyparis leylandii* 'Haggerston Grey' (Leyland cypress): columnar, gray-green foliage, vigorous, fast-growing.

×*Cupressocyparis leylandii* 'Naylor's Blue' (Leyland cypress): vigorous, tall columnar form to 50 ft. (15 m) tall with open branching, gray-blue foliage turns bluer in cold weather, provide good drainage and protection from wind.

Cupressus arizonica 'Blue Ice' (Arizona cypress): upright habit, frosty blue-gray foliage, showy red-brown stems, grows slowly to 15 ft. (4.5 m) tall, wind-tolerant.

Cupressus arizonica 'Blue Pyramid' (Arizona cypress): compact, symmetrical pyramid, silver-gray foliage, reaches 20 to 25 ft. (6 to 8 m) tall.

Cupressus arizonica 'Carolina Sapphire' (Arizona cypress): upright broadly pyramidal form with silver-blue foliage, rapid growing.

Cupressus arizonica 'Sapphire Skies' (Arizona cypress): narrow, pyramidal, rich blue-green foliage.

Cupressus arizonica 'Silver Smoke' (Arizona cypress): narrow with open branching and drooping tips, blue-gray foliage.

Juniper chinensis 'Blue Alps' (Chinese juniper): upright and vigorous spreading shrub with slightly pendulous prickly silvery blue-green foliage, red-brown bark, reaches 20 ft. (6 m) tall by 10 ft. (3 m) wide.

Juniperus chinensis 'Blue Point' (Chinese juniper): conical with dense blue-green foliage, grows to 12 ft. (3.6 m) high and 8 ft. (2.5 m) wide, good for hedges.

Juniperus conferta 'Blue Lagoon' (shore juniper): dense spreading mat of prickly green needles with blue overtones, single white band on each needle, turns plum in winter, grows 1 ft. (0.3 m) tall by 9 ft. (2.7 m) wide.

Juniperus conferta 'Blue Pacific' (shore juniper): spreading mat with prickly foliage, green with blue and silver overtones, does not bronze in winter.

Juniperus conferta 'Silver Mist' (shore juniper): salt-tolerant prostrate form with densely growing intensely silvery blue prickly foliage.

Juniperus horizontalis 'Blue Horizon' (prostrate juniper): low-growing creeping plant, does not mound up, blue-green foliage, bronzing in winter, male.

Juniperus horizontalis 'Blue Rug' (prostrate juniper): one of the best ground-hugging forms, scalelike foliage glaucous blue year-round, female.

Juniperus horizontalis 'Douglasii' (prostrate juniper): wide-spreading and low-growing with mixed foliage, gray-green in summer, bronzed in cold weather, very small needles clasp the stem on semi-erect branchlets, useful in sand gardens.

Juniperus horizontalis 'Icee Blue' (prostrate juniper): the name says it all, reaches 4 in. (10 cm) tall by 8 ft. (2.5 m) wide.

Juniperus scopulorum 'Blue Arrow': compact small tree with a narrow upright habit, 12 to 15 ft. (3.6 to 4.5 m) tall by 2 ft. (0.6 m) wide, blue-gray foliage.

Juniperus scopulorum 'Blue Heaven': erect column, compact rough adult foliage, silver-blue in warm seasons, blue-green in colder, to 6 ft. (1.8 m) tall.

Juniperus scopulorum 'Wichita Blue': loose and irregular open pyramidal habit with ascending branches, intense silver-blue foliage all year, grows to 12 ft. (3.6 m) tall by 6 ft. (1.8 m) wide, male.

Juniperus squamata 'Blue Carpet' (singleseed juniper): fast-growing horizontal sprays, reaching 12 in. (30 cm) tall by 6 ft. (1.8 m) wide, silver-blue foliage turning gray-green in winter, easy to grow.

Juniperus squamata 'Blue Star' (singleseed juniper): irregular slow-growing mound of dense blue foliage changing to a purplish heather-blue in winter, does best in full sun, to 16 in. (40 cm) high, sometimes grafted on standards.

Juniperus squamata 'Blue Star'

Juniperus virginiana 'Grey Owl': soft dusty silver-gray foliage and abundant silver-gray cones, grows slowly into a wide-spreading shrub 3 ft. (0.9 m) tall by 6 ft. (1.8 m) wide, drought tolerant. Exceptional.

Juniperus virginiana 'Silver Spreader': low groundcovering shrub, foliage thick and coarse, bright silver-gray in summer, more gray-green in winter, undemanding.

Larix kaempferi 'Blue Rabbit' (Japanese larch): narrow and conical with blue foliage, reaches 70 ft. (21 m) tall and 15 ft. (4.5 m) wide, often grown on a standard.

Picea glauca 'Sander's Blue' (white spruce): tight conical growth, soft slate-blue foliage, tends to revert to green, use like Alberta white spruce (*P. glauca* 'Conica').

Picea pungens 'Baby Blueyes' (Colorado spruce): slow-growing, dense, symmetrical, and pyramidal with bright blue foliage, slower growing than 'Hoopsii', faster than 'Montgomery'. Stunning.

Picea pungens 'Egyptian Pyramid' (Colorado spruce): dense and broadly pyramidal, to 6 ft. (1.8 m) tall and wide, blue cones.

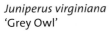

Juniperus virginiana 'Grey Owl'

Left: *Larix kaempferi* 'Blue Rabbit' foliage.

Below: *Picea pungens* 'Egyptian Pyramid'

Picea pungens 'Fat Albert' (Colorado spruce): densely compact, symmetrical with a broad base, soft silvery blue foliage, reaches 15 ft. (4.5 m) tall.

Picea pungens f. *glauca* (Colorado spruce): the common blue spruce, sharp, stiff bluish green needles with the new growth the bluest, often darkens by winter, great variation among specimens.

Picea pungens 'Hoopsii' (Colorado spruce): silvery blue selection, sometimes almost white with long sharp needles, irregular early on but grows into elegance.

Picea pungens 'Hunnewelliana' (Colorado spruce): slow-growing, conical but eventually tall, silver-blue foliage

Picea pungens 'Iseli Fastigiate' (Colorado spruce): narrowly upright, blue foliage, subject to snow damage.

Picea pungens
'Montgomery'

Picea pungens 'Montgomery' (Colorado spruce): compact, broadly pyramidal, silvery blue shrub that grows 3 to 6 in. (7.5 to 15 cm) a year, one of the most commonly grown dwarf Colorado spruces.

Picea pungens 'Thomsen' (Colorado spruce): bright silver-blue thick needles.

Pinus flexilis 'Extra Blue' (limber pine): gray powdery blue needles, 8 ft. (2.5 m) high in 10 years.

Pinus flexilis 'Vanderwolf's Pyramid' (limber pine): some say the best of the blue foliage forms with a dense, uniform habit, 30 to 50 ft.

(9 to 15 m) tall by 20 to 30 ft. (6 to 9 m) wide, grows 2 ft. (0.6 m) a year, adaptable to heat and a wide range of soil conditions.

Pinus parviflora 'Aoi' (Japanese white pine): irregular upright habit, tight bunches of silver-blue needles, popular for bonsai because of its good trunk formation, grows 1 to 1½ in. (2.5 to 3.5 cm) a year.

Pinus parviflora 'Glauca' (Japanese white pine): popular and available, an irregular pyramidal small tree with long twisted silver-blue needles, persistent cones, reaches 6 to 8 ft. (1.8 to 2.5 m) in 10 years.

Pinus parviflora 'Glauca Brevifolia' (Japanese white pine): shorter, more up-curved needles than *P. parviflora* 'Glauca'.

Pinus parviflora 'Watnong' (Japanese white pine): very slow-growing into a regular pyramidal form, often rather full with incurving gray-blue needles.

Pinus strobus 'Blue Shag' (eastern white pine): slow-growing 4 in. (10 cm) a year with a dense, rounded habit and silver-blue needles.

Pinus sylvestris 'Argentea Compacta' (Scots pine): a dense form with silvery foliage, slow-growing only 2 in. (5 cm) a year but can reach 10 ft. (3 m) tall.

Pinus flexilis 'Extra Blue'

Pinus sylvestris 'Waterei' (Scots pine): globose, usually considered a dwarf, only 8 to 12 in. (20 to 30 cm) tall and wide, grows 4 to 6 in. (10 to 15 cm) a year to 12 ft. (3.6 m) high, foliage appears blue.

Pseudotsuga menziesii 'Wycoff's Big Blue' (Douglas-fir): upright and pyramidal, good blue foliage, produces abundant cones, reaches 40 ft. (12 m) tall by 20 ft. (6 m) wide.

Sequoiadendron giganteum 'Hazel Smith' (giant sequoia): gray-blue foliage on uniformly pyramidal tree for the larger landscape, grows 18 in. (46 cm) a year.

Sequoiadendron giganteum 'Powder Blue' (giant sequoia): light blue needles, reaches 12 ft. (3.6 m) tall by 6 ft. (1.8 m) wide in 10 years.

Green Conifers

To **THIS POINT** we have looked at conifers that are useful in designs because their foliage is yellow, gray, blue, or silver, but sometimes the gardener wants a conifer that is simply a rich green. Fortunately, plenty of conifers have green foliage. The trick is to find which of them stay green year-round because some change color during cold seasons.

The eastern arborvitae (*Thuja occidentalis*), also known as northern white-cedar, is one of the most readily available and widely planted of conifers in the home garden where it is commonly used for hedges and screening. However, the foliage tends to turn bronze in the winter. The same is true of the eastern red-cedar (*Juniperus virginiana*) which is often planted because of its drought tolerance and value for birds. Fortunately, both of these species have cultivars that have been specifically introduced because they hold their rich green color all year long.

Aged Japanese-cedars (*Cryptomeria japonica*) not only turn a bronze-green in the winter, but also display patches of brown or dead foliage here and there and these have to be removed. In time these mature trees develop a "poodled" appearance. Again, several superior cultivars are available that stay green throughout the year and maintain their foliage to the ground.

A connoisseur gardener who features a Japanese umbrella-pine (*Sciadopitys verticillata*) will first explain to you that it is not actually a pine and will then want you to check out the luxuriant foliage. Although the fleshy, pliable needles do yellow a bit in the winter to an olive-green shade, one selection remains green year-round.

Year-round Green Conifers

Cryptomeria japonica 'Benjamin Franklin' (Japanese-cedar): vigorous and upright reaching 20 ft. (6 m) tall, salt-tolerant, remains green during the winter.

Cryptomeria japonica 'Black Dragon' (Japanese-cedar): vigorous, dense, upright conical habit to 6 ft. (1.8 m) tall, pale green spring growth ages to deep dark almost black-green in winter.

Cryptomeria japonica
'Black Dragon'

Cryptomeria japonica 'Elegans Viridis' (Japanese-cedar): beautiful feathery foliage, reaches 10 ft. (3 m) tall in 10 years.

Cryptomeria japonica 'Gracilis' (Japanese-cedar): erect and narrow to 16 ft. (5 m) tall, light green all seasons.

Cryptomeria japonica 'Nana' (Japanese-cedar): slow-growing to 3 ft. (0.9 m), horizontal branchlets with drooping tips, green all seasons.

Cryptomeria japonica 'Yoshino' (Japanese-cedar): beautiful pyramidal form reaching 20 ft. (6 m) tall by 8 ft. (2.5 m) wide, growing 1 ft. (0.3 m) a year, retains branches to the ground. Choice.

Juniperus virginiana 'Corcorcor': narrow and conical, remains a rich green all seasons, rapid growing, sturdy and dependable, reaches 25 to 30 ft. (8 to 9 m) tall, also called 'Emerald Sentinel'.

A grove of *Cryptomeria japonica* 'Yoshino' near a pool.

Sciadopitys verticillata 'Wintergreen' (Japanese umbrella-pine): not a true pine despite the common name, foliage remains glossy green through winter.

Thuja 'Green Giant' (arborvitae): tall, narrow, and densely conical hybrid, grows 3 to 5 ft. (0.9 to 1.5 m) a year, reaching 60 ft. (18 m) tall by 20 ft. (6 m) wide, very fast-growing.

Thuja occidentalis 'Degroot's Spire' (eastern arborvitae): slow-growing, narrow and tightly branched, rich green in summer, turning slightly bronze in winter (see photo).

Thuja occidentalis 'Hetz Wintergreen' (eastern arborvitae): vigorous, grows ramrod straight, no snow load or ice problems if trained to

Left: *Juniperus virginiana* 'Corcorcor'

Right: *Sciadopitys verticillata* 'Wintergreen'

Thuja occidentalis 'Hetz Wintergreen'

Opposite: *Thuja occidentalis* 'Smaragd'

a central leader, reaches 35 ft. (10.5 m) tall by 8 ft. (2.5 m) wide in 35 years.

Thuja occidentalis 'Smaragd' (eastern arborvitae): grows rapidly, reaching 15 ft. (4.5 m) tall by 4 ft. (1.2 m) wide in 15 years, stays compact, narrow, and upright, train to a single leader, also listed as 'Emerald Green'.

Thuja plicata 'Virescens' (giant arborvitae): narrow and upright with very glossy foliage, a selection of western arborvitae which is less attractive to deer.

Conifers with Ornamental Bark

NUMEROUS DECIDUOUS SHRUBS are grown for their colorful bark or stems, for instance, the red- and yellow-stemmed dogwoods (*Cornus*), willows (*Salix*), and several species of Japanese maples (*Acer palmatum*). Gardeners do not usually think of planting conifers for their bark; however, a few have attention-getting characteristics and are discussed here.

Araucaria araucana (monkey-puzzle tree)

With age the trunk is described as resembling an elephant's foot. The branches are held in tiers displaying the corky bark with spiny pointed leaves. This tree has viciously prickly, forward-pointing, very stiff needles.

Opposite: *Pinus densiflora*

Araucaria araucana

Metasequoia glyptostroboides (dawn redwood)
The orange to russet-brown bark develops fissures with age and peels in long strips. The base of the trunk becomes buttressed and irregularly fluted. Children know this conifer as the "armpit tree" (see photo).

Pinus bungeana (lacebark pine)
The bark exfoliates in irregular patches of brown, gray, green, and white after the tree is five to eight years old. Very old trees become bone white.

Pinus densiflora (Japanese red pine)
The bark is orangish to orange-red or bright reddish brown and flaking. Old trees display scaly gray plates with deep reddish furrows.

Left: *Pinus bungeana*

Right: *Pinus sylvestris*

Pinus sylvestris (Scots pine)

Stems up to 12 in. (30 cm) in diameter have a thin orange scaly bark that exfoliates in small, irregular papery plates. The bark is very noticeable since the trees are often high branched.

Sequoiadendron giganteum (giant sequoia)

The spongy bark is a rich red-brown and can be up to 12 in. (30 cm) thick, or even thicker on mature specimens, with deep furrows and fibrous ridges. It is soft and easily hollowed out by birds and squirrels.

Taxodium distichum (bald-cypress)

The fibrous reddish brown bark peels off in thin, narrow strips. It weathers to a brownish gray.

Left: *Sequoiadendron giganteum*

Right: *Taxodium distichum*

Taxus baccata (English yew)

The bark is reddish to dark chestnut-brown and exfoliates from the trunk and larger branches in long, thin strips revealing purple-red patches.

Thuja plicata (giant arborvitae, western red-cedar)

In its native forests this arborvitae forms a magnificent tree with a stout buttressed trunk clad in thin, red-brown to gray-brown bark. With age the fibrous and shredding bark forms narrow flat ridges.

Taxus baccata

Thuja plicata

Deciduous Conifers for Fall Color

WHY WOULD ANYONE WANT TO GROW a *deciduous* conifer? Don't we love conifers because they *don't* lose their leaves?

Many people are not aware that some conifers actually lose their leaves in the fall. Or rather, many people are not aware that several trees they have admired, like the bald-cypress (*Taxodium distichum*) or dawn redwood (*Metasequoia glyptostroboides*), are actually, botanically, conifers. As such, these trees are related to junipers (*Juniperus*) and arborvitae (*Thuja*). The other deciduous conifers, larch (*Larix*) and golden-larch (*Pseudolarix*), are cousins of the pines (*Pinus*).

Deciduous conifers have a lot to offer even in gardens with other fine shade trees that lose their leaves like oaks (*Quercus*), maples (*Acer*), and lindens (*Tilia*).

Ginkgo biloba (maidenhair tree)

Most people know that the ginkgo was growing on earth long before the time of the dinosaurs. Today we continue to cultivate it in urban

Opposite: *Taxodium distichum* in fall color

Ginkgo biloba fall color

areas and home gardens because it is such a tough and durable tree. It is dioecious, meaning that some trees (male) produce pollen-bearing cones while other trees (female) produce seed-bearing cones. The fleshy "fruit" of the female trees is messy and rank smelling. Although trees have to be decades old before they produce the cones, it is advisable to plant a male selection. The shape of the leaves is like no other tree and the fall color a clear yellow.

Larix (larch)

Several *Larix* species are widely distributed in the colder sections of the Northern Hemisphere. Their great attraction to the home gardener is their lime green foliage that emerges early in the spring, their golden flash of fall color, and, in some cases, their austere winter habit. A choice selection for the home garden is a shrubby weeping form of European larch, *L. decidua* 'Puli'

Metasequoia glyptostroboides (dawn redwood)

Dawn redwood has a tongue-twister Latin name but is an outstanding specimen tree for the gardener who has room for it. It rapidly reaches 40 to 50 ft. (12 to 15 m) tall in fewer than 20 years. This very orderly and uniform tree has a sharply pointed top on a central single stem.

Right: *Larix decidua* 'Puli'

Opposite, top: A grove of *Metasequoia glyptostroboides*.

Opposite, bottom left: Fall color of *Metasequoia glyptostroboides*.

Opposite, bottom right: Foliage of *Metasequoia glyptostroboides* 'Ogon'.

The leaves are bright green when they emerge and have a ferny texture through the growing season. In fall the color changes from a yellow-brown to pink, even apricot, then a copper-brown. The tree tolerates very wet, even boggy soil for part of the year and is fine with urban conditions. The trunk is buttressed with age; children love it and call it the "armpit tree." A choice option for any landscape is 'Ogon', which has golden-yellow foliage throughout the entire summer.

Pseudolarix amabilis (golden-larch)

Many observers agree that the foliage of the golden-larch is the most eye-catching of any conifer. The mint-green leaves emerge in early spring and unfold into soft, feathery, whorled, flat needles. They turn a dazzling golden orange in the fall. The tree appears as if it is lighted from within. No worries about this tree outgrowing its space; it grows very slowly and takes a decade to reach 10 ft. (3 m) tall.

Taxodium distichum (bald-cypress)

Bald-cypress is a tough long-lived native found in swamps from Delaware to Florida, but will also grow fine in dry situations. Of all trees, it has the greatest tolerance for flooding. It is famous for the "knees" that extend from the roots when it is growing by a stream. It produces a russet or soft brown fall color. A particularly nice shrubby form is the pendulous 'Cascade Falls' (see photo).

Left: *Pseudolarix amabilis* foliage

Right: *Taxodium distichum* "knees"

Opposite: *Taxodium distichum*

3

Conifers for Specific Sites and Conditions

Front Gardens

ENTRENCHED IN OUR IMAGINATION and traditions is the notion that our front yard should be an expanse of weed-free green turf with clipped yews and a few spring-flowering azaleas in a row in front of the foundation of the house. Certainly, this is the custom throughout the endless cookie-cutter suburban subdivisions that have cropped up since the middle of the twentieth century. The building contractor typically "installs" the "landscaping," which is usually designed to be viewed from the street. Rarely are plants chosen with a thought to the height and breadth they will have at maturity, nor are plants selected for the grace of their natural unpruned shapes.

But do our contemporary houses need a planting along their foundation at all? Foundation plantings came about during the Victorian era when huge homes sitting on massive foundations with high porches to front, side, or rear became popular. To anchor the houses and bring them back into scale with their surroundings, homeowners skirted their dwelling with full-size shrubs such as kolkwitzia, philadelphus, lilacs (*Syringa*), yews, and junipers.

As house styles evolved into smaller, lower structures, the rationale for foundation plantings also changed. We continued using them to hide foundations. Many times, though, the typical ring-around-the-house plantings using the same big shrubs just created work keeping everything in bounds. Today most foundations look pretty good, actually, and the bottom course of siding is close to the ground. Even so, we still put in foundation plantings. We're so accustomed to the style that our homes look naked without them.

Oddly enough, the front of the house is often the only place we think of putting a shrub border, even though a site on the edge of the lawn, with plenty of room for the shrubs to spread out naturally, might be better. Furthermore, all too often the foundation planting is considered the "garden" and is only area that gets attention (along with the turf, of course).

Why this mandatory dress code? It is time to break free of this tradition and change our practices.

Some modern-day designers refer to the area in front of the house

Overleaf: *Juniperus virginiana* 'Grey Owl' and *Pinus sylvestris* 'Glauca' trained 40 years.

Opposite: This front garden pushes exuberance to its limit (perhaps even beyond), but it does show the variety that can be achieved with conifers.

An example of the kind of typical foundation planting used in front of so many houses. The lack of imagination displayed here gives conifers a bad name.

Below: Cedars (*Cedrus*) are readily available and appealing but usually, like the species and pendulous forms here, are planted too close to structures.

as the "welcoming garden." Today we are becoming more interested in blending the house with the setting so that it looks natural. An island planting set away from the house or along a winding path leading up to it can be much more inviting than plants set in a row all the way across the front of the house. Maybe a terrace or a curved entrance walkway would be nice directly in front. Instead of walking past a row of green blobs, why not have arriving guests walk *among* plants and even pause on the way to the door? With some imagination the front area of a home can become a dynamic garden space to be enjoyed rather than merely a static view to be observed.

Slow-growing conifers are ideal for use in front gardens because they won't outgrow their space for many years, they provide year-round presence, and they require minimal maintenance. Far from being curiosities for knowledgeable collectors, there are many readily available cultivars that will mix easily with bulbs, annuals, and herbaceous plants to give pleasure to the homeowner and guests.

The entrance planting surrounding the stone steps and graceful iron railing creates a sense of privacy, and even of mystery.

The combination of conifers with sturdy herbaceous plants provides a very attractive solution to a steep slope near a sunroom addition.

Opposite, top: Although the conifers in this suburban setting are large, they are far enough from the houses that they don't seem out of scale.

Opposite, bottom: Every inch of soil is imaginatively planted in this tiny urban garden.

Opposite, top: A formal approach to frontside plantings.

Opposite, bottom: Parking strip plantings of an avid gardener with a lenient town council. Before attempting something similar, be sure to consider vehicle traffic, pedestrian traffic, snow plows, salt spray, shade trees, root systems, and utility lines. And, of course, local regulations governing the area between the sidewalk and the street.

Hedges and Screens

ALTHOUGH WALLS AND FENCES can be constructed to form permanent boundaries and divisions around and within the garden, living hedges often look more attractive. Hedges define space and create rooms within a large garden. Nothing looks as great as a dense, dark green clipped hedge behind a border of colorful flowering plants or providing an alcove for a bench, sculpture, or fountain.

So much of what we like about some gardens—the sense of mystery and discovery and the feeling of being enclosed in a private world—is the result of hedging.

Hedges can also act as barriers to keep out people or animals or serve as screens to hide unwanted views and create privacy. They are often used to define property lines where they are more effective as an impediment to wind, noise, and pollution than fences, and provide

Opposite: The tall arbor-vitae hedge here creates a garden room.

A tall hedge provides a background for exuberant plantings and screens business-related equipment.

Opposite, top: The gardens of royalty proclaimed the power of humans over nature at Herrenhausen Gardens in Hannover, Germany.

Opposite, bottom: An example of an elaborate parterre at Herrenhausen using arborvitae (*Thuja*).

protective cover and nesting site for birds. Some gardeners establish enclosing hedges to create a protective microclimate locale for experimenting with plants that are not ordinarily hardy in their area.

Moreover, hedges are enormously flexible in terms of space. They can be merely edging plants barely a foot (30 cm) high or towering trees in a shelter belt.

The hedgerow has been a feature of the landscape in Europe since medieval times. There are English manor houses with yew hedges that are hundreds of years old. Monastery gardens, usually places where medicinal plants were cultivated, were typically enclosed by a hedge. The vast gardens of royalty in France, Germany, and Italy often used trimmed large trees to outline sections and line carriage paths. Often they display a symmetry that focuses the viewer's gaze onto a particular spot. Or they can surround circular pools, or be trained into loops and curls in a knot pattern known as a parterre.

Pruning a Hedge

Obviously the planting of a row of identical trees in an unnaturally close spacing to give the effect of one long narrow plant is not a normal way for conifers to grow. Fortunately, the growth and shape of many conifers can be trained by pruning or shearing. Some plants can be manipulated into round, square, globular, or any shape desired.

The best conifers for hedging are those that will sprout readily when they are cut. For this characteristic, nothing compares with yew (*Taxus*). Yew can be cut back to the trunk and will sprout again. It is possible, moreover desirable, to rejuvenate very old yew hedges for that reason. Other conifers discussed in this chapter will accept vigorous shearing and resprout, but not cutting all the way back to old wood.

To be done well, pruning requires knowledge of proper pruning methods along with a steady hand, an artistic eye, and a respect for safety precautions. The more often the sides of a young hedge are trimmed, within reason, the better. There's no getting around the fact that hedges are labor intensive. The idea is to encourage the hedge to sprout repeatedly until it forms a dense thicket of twigs. The top is left to grow straight up until it reaches the height desired, then trimmed along with the sides. The lines of formal pruning of hedges and screens should be crisp, whether straight or curved.

A basic rule for trimming formal hedges that is seldom observed is that the shape should be wider at the bottom and narrower at the top

to allow sunlight to reach the lower leaves. Otherwise the lower section of the hedge will lose foliage from lack of sunlight and be unsightly. This contour will also insure less damage to the plants with heavy snowfall. Be prepared to take two to three years to train a hedge, even with fast-growing cultivars. How often an established formal hedge requires pruning is determined by the growth characteristics of the conifer and the shape of the hedge.

A hedge with a proper slope, also known as a "batter."

Spruce, fir, and pine should only be trimmed in spring when active new growth is in progress. About half of the new growth can be trimmed to keep the plant more compact and the plant will set buds for the following year's growth during the season. Arborvitae can be trimmed any time of the year since it continuously puts on new growth. If it is sheared rather than pruned carefully with hand pruners, it will show some browning where it has been cut. Shearing early in the season, however, will allow the vigorous new growth to hide any browning. Yew is best pruned after it has finished the new growth in the spring, but summer and fall trimming is fine also.

To prune a large hedge, place poles in the ground along one side within the hedge. Run a taut string between the poles to provide a straight edge as a guide. It is important to wear protective goggles and sturdy gloves with long cuffs. Special care is advised when working from a ladder.

Selecting Conifers for Hedging

When selecting conifers for hedging, be sure the species is suitable culturally for the site conditions you have and will provide the texture you want. It is especially important to know the growth rate because this will determine how long it will take to establish the size you need and, even more pertinent once the hedge is established, how often during the busy gardening season trimming will have to be done.

The gardener or designer with a sizeable budget will be tempted to order plants at the nursery which are very large so that an instant effect is achieved. This is not a good plan. Smaller plants, around 12 to 20 in. (30 to 50 cm) tall, are not only cheaper but will usually establish themselves much more quickly than older specimens as they grow roots in the soil in which they are planted.

Another recommendation, appropriate for lower hedges or barriers is to select upright, relatively slow-growing cultivars with a dense compact habit, plant them close together, and let them grow into a maintenance-free hedge.

Be aware that the color of the needled or scalelike foliage of some genera will change slightly during the course of fall and winter in colder climates. Some will darken; others might take on a yellow-green or bronze color. There are a few that will change from a yellow-green to a bright gold; these are often grown as specimens.

You'll also need to know the locations of underground electric lines, cables, and water pipes so you can avoid them.

Selecting Conifers for Screens

With "hedge" we usually are thinking of a planting where the growth is controlled by shearing to produce a compact, often very geometrical form. With "screen" we are referring to the purpose of a planting: to block unwanted views, filter out noise or pollution, or act as a barrier to persons or animals.

Although it goes against what one thinks of as a hedge, if the main purpose is to screen a view, it is a good idea to grow a mixed hedge: simply a row of closely planted deciduous and evergreen plants. Using a variety of species will mean the hedge is healthier. In a sizeable hedge comprised of only one species, a pest or disease can afflict the entire planting and result in the removal of an entire screen that might have taken years to develop.

Suitable groundcovers can be planted in a mixed hedge to obscure

Opposite, top: A gold-foliaged arborvitae (*Thuja*) hedge separates a garden from the street. The tree is a monkey-puzzle (*Araucaria araucana*).

Opposite, bottom: Tall and low hedges define spaces for colorful annual displays in a public garden.

Below: This dense mixed border efficiently screens the house from traffic and the gaze of passers-by.

any legginess an occasional selection might have. A screen that is created using a variety of conifers will have a less formal and more natural appearance because plants are allowed to assume their natural growth habits. Privacy is provided without requiring the constant maintenance needed by a formal hedge.

Calocedrus decurrens (incense-cedar)

Incense-cedar has a naturally slender shape with abruptly ascending branches making it a reasonable choice for a large hedge or screen. Left unpruned, the symmetrically columnar tree grows to 40 ft. (12 m) tall. It is both heat-tolerant and very drought-tolerant (see photo).

Chamaecyparis (false cypress)

There is a false-cypress available to fill practically any landscape requirement a gardener could think of, and they are easy to transplant. Numerous cultivars are ideal for hedging. Two selections of *Chamaecyparis lawsoniana* (Lawson false cypress) are among them. 'Green Hedger' is a uniform-growing, dense, erect pyramidal form with

Opposite, top: In larger properties, conifer screens can include species, such as the common Colorado blue spruce (*Picea pungens*), that would be disastrously out of scale on a small city or suburban lot.

Opposite, bottom: Mature conifers provide privacy around a swimming pool.

Below: A slow-growing cultivar of *Chamaecyparis obtusa* provides a maintenance-free hedge.

bright green foliage; it branches from the base. 'Columnaris' is a tight narrow column that grows 15 to 20 ft. (4.5 to 6 m) tall; it has blue-green foliage in dense flat sprays. *Chamaecyparis obtusa* (hinoki false cypress) has countless medium-sized, slow-growing selections that can be grown as a low compact hedge.

Chamaecyparis lawsoniana 'Green Hedger'

×*Cupressocyparis leylandii* (Leyland cypress)

The feathery soft foliage of this drought- and salt-tolerant conifer will thicken to create a solid wall that stays green year-round. Space plants for a hedge 6 ft. (1.8 m) apart. This intergeneric hybrid is popular for the very reason that makes it a tricky customer—its incredible growth rate of 3 to 4 ft. (0.9 to 1.2 m) per year, which means it will soon be out of the unwary gardener's control. It can be pruned quite severely.

It is widely planted in the British Isles, where it grows so well that it has sparked court cases when the tall plants have been allowed to block light to a neighbor's garden and obstruct views. It is truly an "instant hedge" selection, but the homeowner needs to be aware that if it is allowed to grow as a very tall screen it will shade out the lower branches and the bottom growth will be thin and unattractive.

Large hedges will naturally have substantial root systems which will cause dryness in the area making it difficult to plant a flower

A display hedge with several Leyland cypress (×*Cupressocyparis leylandii*) cultivars.

border without supplemental irrigation. It is wise to select small container-grown specimens and plant them in the spring. This allows the plants to distribute their fibrous roots in the soil. Larger specimens planted in the fall in exposed sites are subject to heaving out of frozen soil or being blown over by winds.

Four cultivars are worth mentioning here. Popular in England, 'Castlewellan Gold' can reach 16 ft. (4.9 m) tall in the first 10 years and has a spread of 7 to 15 ft. (2 to 4.5 m); it is best in a sunny location to maintain golden color. 'Leighton Green' is one of the fastest growing Leyland cultivars, reaching 40 ft. (12 m) tall; it is excellent trimmed into a formal hedge. 'Naylor's Blue' has gray-blue foliage that is pendulous at the tips, and 'Star Wars' is a white-variegated form.

Cupressus (cypress)

Cypresses are very tolerant of hot dry condition and require full sun. Generally fast-growing, they are suitable for seashore plantings since they tolerate poor sandy soils. It is best to provide shelter from harsh winds.

Cupressus arizonica (Arizona cypress) has two noteworthy cultivars: 'Blue Ice', with beautiful frosty blue-gray aromatic foliage, an upright habit, and showy red-brown stems, grows slowly to 15 ft. (4.5 m) and is wind-tolerant (see photo). 'Carolina Sapphire' tolerates heat, drought, and poor soil, has silver-blue foliage, and grows 3 ft. (0.9 m) a year.

Cupressus macrocarpa (Monterey cypress) is a naturally uniform tree, drought-tolerant tree which forms a great hedge because it trims well. Elegant and narrow, this columnar, not pyramidal, cypress, grows 2 to 3 ft. (0.6 to 0.9 m) a year. It can also be used to frame an entrance, cover up utility poles, or soften corners. Monterey cypress can be topped at any height.

Cryptomeria japonica (Japanese-cedar)

Japanese-cedar is usually grown as an ornamental specimen but can be grown as a screen. It has soft feathery foliage and grows 1 ft. (30 cm) a year. Left unpruned, it reaches 40 ft. (12 m) tall, but it has the ability to regrow and thus can be pruned to 10 ft. (3 m) tall. This elegant conifer tolerates part shade. Two cultivars with year-round green color are the compact 'Radicans' and 'Yoshino' (see photo), the latter growing 12 in. (30 cm) a year and retaining branches to the ground.

Juniperus (juniper)

Like the true cypresses, many junipers come from hot dry climates and are tolerant of a wide range of sites provided they have full sun and good drainage. Many are even tolerant of alkaline soils. Junipers can withstand shaping for development into hedges. 'Spartan', a fast-growing selection of *Juniperus chinensis* (Chinese juniper), forms a dense narrow column to 16 ft. (5 m) tall and has rich dark green foliage; it is tolerant to heat, cold, drought, and salt and makes a good wind barrier. 'Skyrocket', a very narrow selection of *J. scopulorum* (Rocky Mountain juniper), grows to 15 ft. (4.5 ft.) tall by 2 ft. (0.6 m) wide; the blue-green foliage darkens in winter.

Three selections of *Juniperus virginiana* (eastern red-cedar) are

Juniperus virginiana 'Blue Arrow'

suitable for hedging. 'Blue Arrow' has a narrow and upright habit reaching 6 ft. (1.8 m) tall in 10 years; it retains its lower branches and has deep blue foliage. 'Burkii' is columnar with a straight stem and ascending branches, reaches 6 ft. (1.8 m) in 10 years, and has dense blue-green foliage that bronzes in winter. 'Corcorcor' is narrow and conical, reaching 25 to 30 ft. (8 to 9 m) tall; sturdy and dependable, it maintains its rich-green foliage all seasons and is also called 'Emerald Sentinel' (see photo).

Taxodium (bald-cypress)

Bald-cypress is tolerant of very wet conditions and is most often grown as a specimen or in a grove under those conditions. The recent introduction of columnar and slow-growing cultivars makes it worthy of consideration for use as a deciduous hedge in an area subject to flooding.

Unusual, a clipped bald-cypress (*Taxodium*) hedge for a large space, behind the low yew (*Taxus*) hedge in a public garden

Taxus (yew)

Yews are the foremost conifers for hedging. Tolerant of most well-drained soils, they are even tolerant of considerable shade, but they are not tolerant of salt. The foliage, bark, and seeds are very poisonous to farm livestock (not to mention human beings), but not to moose, elk, or deer. Suburban gardeners are well aware of the special fondness of white-tailed deer for yew hedges.

Many cultivars of yew can be used for hedging. Three selections of *Taxus baccata* (English yew) are 'David', an upright form with yellow needles; 'Fastigiata', a fast-growing markedly upright, dense broad column to 30 ft. (9 m) tall with black-green needles (see photo); and 'Standishii', a dense, slow-growing column to 15 ft. (4.5 m) of tightly packed branches with golden-yellow foliage (see photo).

Taxus cuspidata 'Columnaris', a selection of Japanese yew, quickly

A hedge of *Taxus ×media* 'Hicksii'.

produces a dense hedge; it has an upright, narrow habit, stays full at the base, and reaches 10 to 12 ft. (3 to 3.6 m) tall.

Two cultivars of *Taxus ×media* (hybrid yew) with dark green needles are among those suitable for hedges. 'Flushing' has an upright, narrow columnar habit and reaches 12 to 15 ft. (3.6 to 4.5 m) tall but only 3 ft. (0.9 m) wide; it is tolerant of deep shade and must have good drainage (see photo). The fast-growing and erect 'Hicksii' can reach 20 ft. (6 m) tall after many years but is usually pruned; it is excellent.

Thuja (arborvitae)

Thuja 'Green Giant', a compact hybrid with year-round green foliage, has a uniform shape and height. It makes a thick screen with a mature width of 5 ft. (1.5 m) when grown in a row, up to 15 ft. (4.5 m) when grown alone. Easy and adaptable, it has no significant insect or disease problems. It resists ice and snow damage in winter, grows in sandy loam or heavy clay, and accepts a little shade. For a thick barrier, space plants every 6 ft. (1.8 m). This hybrid plant is grown from

Below: A *Thuja occidentalis* 'Smaragd' hedge being established.

Opposite, top: A *Thuja plicata* hedge.

Opposite, bottom: An informal hedge with a golden *Thuja*.

rooting branch cuttings. Make sure the roots are well established. It grows 3 to 5 ft. (0.9 to 1.5 m) per year.

One compact selection of *Thuja occidentalis* (eastern arborvitae, northern white-cedar) has year-round green foliage. 'Smaragd', also listed as 'Emerald Green' is a good choice for smaller yards or tight areas, and also makes an attractive specimen tree. For a neat hedge that requires very little trimming, space plants every 3 to 4 ft. (0.9 to 1.2 m). The foliage is said not to brown even in coldest of winters.

Thuja plicata (giant arborvitae, western red-cedar) forms a broadly conical tree to more than 16 ft. (4.9 m) tall in 10 years. Deer do not browse it as readily as they do eastern arborvitae. Three selections with year-round color are 'Fastigiata', a dense and compact form with slender ascending branches, to 40 ft. (12 m) tall and only 10 ft. (3 m) wide; 'Winter Green' with deep green foliage; and the elegant 'Zebrina', a fast-growing, broadly conical tree with green and gold striped foliage that reaches over 16 ft. (4.9 m) tall in the first 10 years (see photo).

Tsuga canadensis (eastern hemlock)

With soft needles on slender twigs, this shade-tolerant conifer makes an elegant, fine-textured hedge, but sadly can no longer be recommended because of woolly adelgid insect infestation over most of its native range. Existing hedges require regular treatment with horticultural oil if they are to survive over the long term.

Opposite: A double hemlock (*Tsuga*) hedge encloses a formal circular planting

Topiary

TOPIARY IS THE PRUNING and training of plants into unnatural geometric or even fantastic shapes. Gardeners tend to either love or loathe it.

Although the seventeenth century is usually referred to as the golden age of topiary, the use of clipped trees and shrubs in gardens can be traced back to the ancient Egyptians and Persians who introduced the art to the Romans. After the collapse of the Roman Empire in Italy the monks kept the art alive in their enclosed cloisters which included topiary and where they grew medicinal and culinary herbs in knot gardens and among parterres.

During the renaissance the royal heads of Europe and the well-to-do began to build elaborate gardens on their estates. By the early sixteenth century the idea of using hedges to give formal structure culminated in the work of André le Nôtre's designs for the hedging and topiaries of King Louis XIV at the Palace of Versailles outside of Paris, starting in 1661. This style spread across Europe to the gardens of the upper classes throughout the seventeenth century, especially in Germany, and eventually to Great Britain, where mazes and labyrinths had long been popular. There was a period when they fell out of style because of the influence of Lancelot "Capability" Brown's rural landscape style. However many cottage gardens continued to cultivate small topiaries and a revival of interest in creating gardens of trained plants returned by the middle of the nineteenth century.

The Victorians utilized sculptured plants in their exotic plantings and in the twentieth century topiary can be seen in many British gardens popular with the public including Hidcote Manor in Gloucestershire, Levens Hall in Cumbria, Sissinghurst Castle in Kent, and Great Dixter in East Sussex.

In the United States topiary has enjoyed a continued popularity. Public displays of topiary are notable at Longwood Gardens in Pennsylvania, Ladew Topiary garden in Monkton, Maryland, Green Animals in Providence, Rhode Island, and, not to be overlooked, at Disneyland. Topiary is popular with the twenty-first century's minimalist modern designs, where, for example, the courtyard "garden" in front

Opposite: Pre-formed topiaries being developed in a nursery. While buying a topiary already made dispenses with the long training period, the plants still need to be maintained.

of a steel and concrete building features water spewing out of a wall and simple yew globes, boxes, or standards.

Large topiary displays involve years of skilled training and pruning to produce figures such as animals and a wide range of architectural and sculptural forms. The care of very old and valuable specimens is best left to the experts.

Nonetheless, the home gardener can enjoy creating topiaries as accents in the garden or perhaps in a patio container. Simple shapes like cones, pyramids, and globes are ideal for the beginner to tackle. Sticks or bamboo stakes can be used as guides for straight-edged designs. With balls and globes it is recommended to start clipping around the "equator" to define the shape before completing the spheres. Elaborate shapes need to be done by eye. Spiral forms are popular but are

Opposite: Topiary at Crathes Castle, Scotland, planted in the eighteenth century. Old topiaries sometimes acquire an almost abstract form.

Below: A topiary garden of yews trained into architectural forms at Longwood Gardens, Pennsylvania.

Above: Here topiary combines with a geometrical parterre and bedding plants in a royal garden in Prague.

Opposite, top: A modern *Thuja* maze. Strictly speaking, a maze is simply a continuous hedge, but from certain vantage points can assume a sculptural quality.

Opposite, bottom: Victorian-style topiary. Spiral topiaries are among the most difficult to maintain, requiring many years of careful clipping and shearing.

challenging for the novice to fashion. The main qualification for designing and executing topiary is plenty of patience and a good set of pruners (or secateurs if you are British!).

Many plants can be trimmed and shaped, but the best choices for such displays are boxwood (*Buxus*), not a conifer, and yew (*Taxus*). Among the conifers, hemlock (*Tsuga*) and arborvitae (*Thuja*) are also frequently used. Yews are ideal because of their vigor, the dark green color of their needles, and their long life. Yew trees can live a thousand years. While boxwoods are less hardy than yews, the former are not browsed by deer, whereas the latter are unfortunately among their favorite treats. Although snow looks very pretty on sculpted conifers, it should be shaken off with a broom rather than risking damage from the weight.

Opposite, top: Whimsical topiary is a hallmark of nineteenth-century cottage gardens, but appears in a starkly modern context at Iseli Nursery, Portland, Oregon.

Opposite, bottom: Spherical clipped yews soften the hardscape and guide the visitor through a round arch to the herbs and roses beyond.

Dwarf Conifers for Containers, Troughs, and Garden Beds

It IS SOMETIMES HARD for gardeners accustomed to growing herbaceous plants to realize that a slow-growing cultivar of a Norway spruce (*Picea abies*) that is only 24 in. (61 cm) tall after several decades is the same species as the 100 ft. (30.5 m) tall spruce towering over their house. Unlike bonsai, these slower-growing selections are naturally small plants. They originate from genetic mutations and are propagated by grafting or rooted cuttings. They look just like their cousins in the landscape but their small scale allows them to be planted in containers or used in garden borders. The availability of these conifers has grown dramatically in recent years and their popularity is surging. The ways these slow-growing conifers can be used in design is only limited by the imagination of the gardener.

All of the little gems described in this chapter are being supplied currently by wholesale growers and should be available on request at better garden centers and definitely from specialty mail-order nurseries. It is important to keep in mind that conifers identified as growing 1 to 6 in. (2.5 to 20 cm) per year will reach 1 to 6 ft. (0.3 to 1.8 m) by age 10 and can be 12 to 15 ft. (3.6 to 4.5 m) when they are 30 or 40 years old. Visitors will often think labels are incorrect when they see "dwarf" cultivars that were planted in public gardens decades earlier.

Trough Gardens

Trough gardens have been popular in England for over a century. Old manor houses had stone sinks and the barns on old estates had stone water troughs for the horses. When these were replaced by metal appliances, the possibility of using them for planting miniature gardens was discovered. These days such stone troughs are hard to find on this side of the pond but the interest in creating "gardens" in troughs and containers of all sizes has only increased. They are attractive displayed on patios surrounded by other plants or assembled in little villages of troughs. Planting a trough garden is an excellent way to enjoy cultivating conifers in a very small area—a miniature garden within a garden. Because they can be displayed on a raised bench, this form of

Opposite: Dwarf conifers in a readily available container.

Opposite, top: Dwarf conifers are indispensable in rock gardens.

Opposite, bottom: A collection of troughs, attractively grouped in a gravel garden at Iseli Nursery, Portland, Oregon.

Left: None of the plants here are rare or unusual, but they gain in effect thanks to the natural stone trough.

Below: A highly pleasing combination of textures and shapes. Conifers featured in the trough are a miniature upright yew (*Taxus baccata* 'Fastigiata Micro'), a rounded Colorado blue spruce (*Picea pungens* 'Gotelli Broom') to its left, and a golden prostrate juniper (*Juniperus horizontalis* 'Mother Lode') in the foreground. Filling the spaces between are a variety of sedums and saxifrages, Japanese holly (*Ilex crenata* 'Jersey Jewel'), and a miniature Chinese elm (*Ulmus parviflora* 'Hokkaido'). To the right of the trough in the background is an eastern white pine (*Pinus strobus* 'Brevifolia Densa').

Picea pungens 'Montgomery' growing in stone trough. The large piece of dead wood is almost sculptural.

Right: Stones and pieces of dead wood can add interest to trough plantings.

Opposite: An unusual vertical garden of dwarf conifers. The concrete uprights hold the stones in place, and the conifers are planted in the cracks.

gardening is ideal for a gardener with disabilities or limited mobility. It is also an opportunity for those living in apartments (flats) or condominiums with a balcony or porch and restrictions about ground planting to grow conifers.

The troughs themselves are often made by the gardener or a group of gardeners working together. Recipes for making authentic-appearing but lightweight "stone" containers out of cement, perlite, and peat (hypertufa) are available from Rock and Alpine Garden Society websites. Numerous lists can be had from these websites also of alpine and other diminutive herbaceous plants that are suitable for these small-scale gardens. However, the suggestions for conifers seldom go beyond a little spiky juniper. There are scores of cultivars of the major conifer genera that can be used even in troughs of a size that only the very slowest growing of conifers should be considered.

Conifers in Pots

Many conifer species can be displayed in ceramic, fiberglass, wood, concrete, or plastic containers which are available in unlimited sizes, shapes, colors, and materials. Container gardening makes it possible even for those living in colder climates to grow unusual species that are not considered hardy in their area. The plants can be enjoyed grouped around the patio or displayed on a stone wall during the spring and summer and then protected in a partially heated well-lit building over winter.

Container plantings do require attention; they will need watering more frequently than in-ground plants during dry spells. Depending on the plantings, some containers will need winter protection. Enthusiasts often cover their troughs with leaves or mulch.

Dwarf conifers tend to be more expensive than landscape-sized plants because of their slow growth rate and longer growing time after rooting or grafting to reach a saleable size. But their lower maintenance makes them ideal for containers or areas of the garden with limited space.

Conifers for Small Containers and Trough Gardens

The conifers in this list are very slow growing, generally less than 2 in. (5 cm) per year.

Abies balsamea 'Nana' (balsam fir): rounded and compact.

Abies koreana 'Silberperl' (Korean fir): congested, wider than tall, short needles with silver undersides and buds that look like silver pearls in fall and winter.

Abies procera 'Blaue Hexe' (noble fir): broad, flat, spherical habit, short, powder blue needles.

Cedrus deodara 'Pygmy' (deodar cedar): extremely slow growing, blue-green needles.

Cedrus libani 'Green Prince' (cedar of Lebanon): deep green needles, becomes an open-branched pyramid giving the appearance of great age, excellent choice for trough garden or bonsai.

Chamaecyparis obtusa 'Elf' (hinoki false cypress): fine-textured with ascending main branches, reaches only 4 in. (5 cm).

Chamaecyparis obtusa 'Gold Drop' (hinoki false cypress): compact and rounded, yellow-green, brighter in winter.

Chamaecyparis obtusa 'Gold Drop'

Chamaecyparis pisifera 'Tsukumo' (sawara-cypress): congested mound, dark green, forms a stout trunk.

Cryptomeria japonica 'Birodo' (Japanese-cedar): globose and compact, medium green in summer, turning purple in winter.

Juniperus communis 'Compressa' (common juniper): narrow upright, cone-shaped without shearing, fine-textured silver blue-green foliage.

Juniperus horizontalis 'Mother Lode' (prostrate juniper): groundcover, brilliant gold in summer turning to shades of deep gold and salmon-orange with green overtones in winter, suitable for hot, sunny, well-drained south-facing sites (see photo).

Picea abies 'Little Gem' (Norway spruce): tight flat dome of dense branches with small light green soft needles. Outstanding.

Picea abies 'Pumila' (Norway spruce): dense flat-topped groundhugging mound, shiny green foliage.

Picea glauca 'Cecilia' (white spruce): compact with short glossy dense silver-blue needles, flat and spreading.

Picea glauca 'Pixie' (white spruce): upright narrow cone with dark green needles, takes 10 years to reach 12 in. (30 cm) (see photo).

Left: *Cryptomeria japonica* 'Birodo'

Right: *Picea abies* 'Little Gem'

Left: *Picea omorika* 'Gunter'

Right: *Pinus leucodermis* 'Compact Gem'

Picea glauca 'Pixie Dust' (white spruce): dense and compact, emerging bud growth is yellow, reaches 16 in. (40 cm) in 10 years (see photo).

Picea omorika 'Gunter' (Serbian spruce): mounding, blue-green foliage.

Picea omorika 'Pimoko' (Serbian spruce): broad-growing bun, short blue-green needles with silver undersides on short branches.

Picea orientalis 'Tom Thumb' (oriental spruce): globose, gold, protect from afternoon sun.

Pinus banksiana 'Chippewa' (jack pine): flat-topped mound, grows less than 1 in. (2.5 cm) a year.

Pinus leucodermis 'Compact Gem' (Bosnian pine): slender, dense, compact, conical shape, drought- and salt-tolerant.

Pinus leucodermis 'Smidtii' (Bosnian pine): dark green, dense and compact, grows under 1 in. (2.5 cm) a year.

Pinus mugo 'Jakobsen' (mugo pine): rounded, grows 1.5 in. (4 cm) a year, dark green congested needles (see photo).

Pinus mugo 'Mitsch Mini' (mugo pine): one of the best bun-shaped mugos, short dark green twisted needles, very salt-tolerant.

Pinus mugo 'Mops' (mugo pine): formal, compact and globose, bright green needles yellow a bit in winter.

Pinus mugo 'Paul's Dwarf' (mugo pine): upright irregular with very short needles, can be candled in spring and kept tiny.

Pinus mugo 'Sherwood Compact' (mugo pine): globular, dark green all seasons with showy buds.

Pinus mugo 'Slowmound' (mugo pine): uniform flat carpet of upward-facing shoots, 1 to 2 ft. (0.3 to 0.6 m) in 10 years (see photo).

Pinus mugo 'Valley Cushion' (mugo pine): compact, low flat and spreading, slowly reaches 3 ft. (0.9 m) wide but only 3 to 4 in. (7.6 to 10 cm) tall.

Pinus strobus 'Minuta' (eastern white pine): low-growing compact bun with short blue-green needles (see photo).

Pinus strobus 'Sea Urchin' (eastern white pine): blue green, low and mounded, grows 2 in. (5 cm) per year.

Pinus sylvestris 'Repens' (Scots pine): forms a slow-growing low mat that is never over 8 in. (20 cm) high in an irregular outline with dull green needles and large resinous buds.

Left: *Pinus leucodermis* 'Smidtii'

Right: *Pinus strobus* 'Sea Urchin'

Thuja occidentalis 'Gold Drop' (eastern arborvitae): yellow-gold variegation.

Conifers for Larger Containers, Rock Gardens, or Foundation Planting

The conifers listed here are slow-growing, generally less than 6 in. (15 cm) per year.

Abies concolor 'Compacta' (concolor fir): irregularly rounded.
Abies koreana 'Prostrate Beauty' (Korean fir): pest free, gray-green.
Chamaecyparis lawsoniana 'Minima Aurea' (Lawson false cypress): broad cone with soft golden yellow foliage.
Chamaecyparis lawsoniana 'Schneeball' (Lawson false cypress): white variegated, globose.
Chamaecyparis obtusa 'Nana Gracilis' (hinoki false cypress): glossy dark green dense cupped foliage, reaches 3 ft. (0.9 m), beware, often mislabeled.

Chamaecyparis obtusa 'Nana Gracilis'

Chamaecyparis obtusa 'Nana Lutea' (hinoki false cypress): bright yellow in the sun, grows 4 to 6 in. (10 to 15 cm) per year.

Chamaecyparis pisifera 'Aurea Nana' (sawara-cypress): globose, golden foliage.

Chamaecyparis pisifera 'White Pygmy' (sawara-cypress): fine-textured tiny bun with white-tipped foliage, grows slowly to 1 ft. (0.3 m) (see photo).

Chamaecyparis thyoides 'Little Jamie' (Atlantic white-cedar, swamp-cedar): narrow, cone-shaped, light green, turns purple-brown in winter, tough.

Cryptomeria japonica 'Little Champion' (Japanese-cedar): low cushion of apple-green foliage (see photo).

Juniperus procumbens 'Nana' (garden juniper): compact mat with layered branches, prickly foliage, blue-green (see photo).

Juniperus squamata 'Blue Star' (singleseed juniper): irregular mound of dense blue foliage changing to a purplish heather-blue in winter (see photo).

Larix kaempferi 'Blue Dwarf' (Japanese larch): low, short blue-green needles on red shoots, reaches 1 ft. (30 cm) tall by 2 ft. (60 cm) wide in 10 years.

Larix kaempferi 'Nana' (Japanese larch): globose, dense soft green foliage in season, golden yellow in fall.

Picea abies 'Clanbrassiliana' (Norway spruce): dense flat-topped bush, wider than tall, only 3 ft. (0.9 m) tall after decades. Choice.

Picea abies 'Nana' (Norway spruce): dense cone with sharp needles.

Picea abies 'Nidiformis' (bird's nest spruce): dense growth 3 to 6 in. (7.6 to 15 cm) per year, wider than tall.

Picea abies 'Pygmaea' (Norway spruce): variable form, compact, becomes broad and dome-shaped, bright green, reaches 18 in. (46 cm) after many years. Outstanding selection.

Picea glauca 'Jean's Dilly' (white spruce): tailored, dark green, in 20 years will still be under 4 ft. (1.2 m).

Picea glauca 'Rainbow's End' (white spruce): creamy yellow new growth.

Picea glauca 'Sander's Blue' (white spruce): tight conical growth, soft slate-blue foliage but unfortunate tendency to revert to green.

Picea omorika 'Nana' (Serbian spruce): broadly conical shrub with two-toned needles eventually becomes pyramidal, reaches 3 ft. (0.9 m) in 10 years.

Picea orientalis 'Barnes'

Picea orientalis 'Barnes' (oriental spruce): nest like with depression in top, shiny dark green needles.

Picea orientalis 'Nana' (oriental spruce): dense globose form.

Picea pungens 'Montgomery' (Colorado spruce): silvery blue, prickly, compact, broadly pyramidal similar to 'Globosa' (see photo).

Pinus cembra 'Nana' (Swiss stone pine): pyramidal, reaches 24 in. (60 cm) in 10 years.

Pinus parviflora 'Adcock's Dwarf' (Japanese white pine): dense, globose form with short gray-green needles clustered at the branch tips, takes 25 years to reach 3 to 4 ft. (0.9 to 1.2 m).

Pinus strobus 'Blue Shag' (eastern white pine): dense, rounded habit and silver-blue needles, grows 4 in. (10 cm) a year.

Pseudotsuga menziesii 'Little Jon': dense dark green cone, eventually upright, 30 in. (75 cm) in 10 years.

Taxus baccata 'Green Diamond' (English yew): rounded with a flat top, rich dark green.

Taxus cuspidata 'Nana' (Japanese yew): spreading form with dense, dark green needles, male, takes shade.

Thuja occidentalis 'Green Midget' (eastern arborvitae): globose, dark green, ultimately 3 ft. (0.9 m) tall and wide.

Thuja occidentalis 'Golden Tuffet' (eastern arborvitae): pillow-shaped, golden orange foliage looks braided (see photo).

Thuja occidentalis 'Rheingold' (eastern arborvitae): oval or cone-shaped, golden yellow in summer, deep coppery gold in winter, soft juvenile foliage, can be sheared, slow-growing, up to 10 ft. (3 m) tall but usually only 2 ft. (0.6 m).

Thujopsis dolabrata 'Nana' (hiba arborvitae): compact, mounded, bright green foliage turns olive-green in winter.

Tsuga canadensis 'Cole's Prostrate' (eastern hemlock): mat forming with branches extending flat along the ground, silver-gray center branches become exposed with maturity, useful for shady area, takes 20 years to reach 3 ft. (0.9 m) (see photo).

Tsuga canadensis 'Gentsch White' (eastern hemlock): white-tipped or variegated foliage, can be sheared, reaches 2 ft. (0.6 m) tall by 3 ft. (0.9 m) (see photo).

Tsuga canadensis 'Lewis' (eastern hemlock): upright, irregular, dense deep green.

Tsuga canadensis 'Minima' (eastern hemlock): short dense branches gray-green.

Shade

It is unlikely that a plant list for creating a garden in the shade would be topped off with a conifer. Hostas and hellebores, definitely, and, for the connoisseur, actaeas and asarums, but certainly not a pine or spruce.

Nevertheless, there are a few conifers that can be used in north-facing borders or under mature deciduous trees. Moreover, several of these are choice plants. Admittedly all these recommendations are appropriate for filtered sun or high shade, not the shade of a dense canopy.

Now, it can't be denied that shade gardeners are always looking for plants that will flower in the shade. But the principal element of garden design should be the structural plants, not colorful flowers whose brief effects flow with the season. And conifer foliage has its own range of colors, shapes, and textures, which will be evident throughout all the year.

Cephalotaxus harringtonia (Japanese plum-yew)
On first glance, Japanese plum-yew looks like its relative, the common yew (*Taxus baccata*), but it is much larger-leaved, slower-growing, and

Opposite: *Microbiota decussata*

Cephalotaxus harringtonia 'Prostrata'

195

perhaps not so versatile. Despite this, it is an eminently garden-worthy plant and the cultivars are becoming more commonly available. Plum-yews grow in sun or part shade but typically grow best as understory shrubs. They have the huge advantage to the home gardener of not being as palatable to deer as the yews famously are. They tend to tolerate wetter soils than yews. 'Fastigiata' is a markedly upright vase-shaped selection for a more formal design; it has deep green, almost black-green needles arranged spirally around the stem (see photo). Another fastigiated form, 'Korean Gold', has yellow new growth (see photo). 'Prostrata' grows 2 to 3 ft. (0.6 to 0.9 m) tall and wide, and can be used as a specimen in a shady mixed border, as a foundation planting, or as a large-scale groundcover.

Chamaecyparis obtusa (hinoki false cypress)

Hinoki false cypress has a wide variety of cultivars, so many in fact, that there is one available to fill practically any conceivable landscape requirement. The plants display rich dark green foliage held in short, flat sprays. No Asian-style garden would be authentic without the inclusion of this species, and it is a favorite of bonsai and trough-gardening enthusiasts. Plants are generally container-grown by nurseries and are easily transplanted.

'Crippsii' with its golden yellow, ferny frond foliage and good winter color is a good accent plant; it is broadly conical to 15 ft. (4.5 m) tall

A dwarf *Chamaecyparis obtusa* in a shady spot with *Athyrium niponicum* var. *pictum* (Japanese painted fern).

Above: *Chamaecyparis obtusa* 'Crippsii'

Left: *Chamaecyparis obtusa* 'Crippsii' foliage.

by 8 ft. (2.5 m) wide. 'Gracilis' with dense dark-green foliage is a good landscaped-size plant. 'Goldilocks' is similar to 'Gracilis' but smaller. 'Fernspray Gold' is another eye-catcher.

Dense layered forms that grow very slowly and are appropriate for troughs, rock, and alpine gardens are 'Nana', 'Nana Aurea', 'Nana Gracilis' (see photo), and 'Nana Lutea'.

Cryptomeria japonica (Japanese-cedar)

Occasionally referred to as Japanese-cedar, *Cryptomeria japonica* is valuable for the designed landscape because of its graceful habit, shade tolerance, and beautiful foliage. It appreciates well-drained, moist soil, and protection from harsh winter winds. It can be sheared and is not prone to any pests or diseases. The soft, dark green needle-like foliage surrounds green stems on new growth.

Cultivars should be sought out because the species changes color in the winter and sheds patches of brown foliage. One of the best is 'Yoshino' which displays a beautiful pyramidal form that reaches 20 ft. (6 m) tall by 8 ft. (2.5 m) wide, growing 1 ft. (0.3 m) a year. The rich green foliage is displayed year-round and this choice selection retains branches to the ground. 'Benjamin Franklin' is similar. 'Rein's Dense Jade' is an outstanding selection (see photo). 'Sekkan-sugi' can reach 30 ft. (9 m) and has yellow-gold tipped foliage in the summer.

Dwarf, slow-growing cultivars which grow slowly to 3 to 5 ft. (0.9

Left: *Cryptomeria japon-ica* 'Globosa Nana'

Right: *Cryptomeria japonica* 'Little Champion'

Opposite: *Cryptomeria japonica* 'Yoshino'

to 1.5 m) with densely branched, blue-green needles include 'Compacta', 'Elegans Nana', 'Globosa', and 'Globosa Nana'. The soft billowy foliage of these selections turns purple-brown in winter. 'Little Champion' with its apple-green foliage or the tufted 'Pom Pom' would be fitting for a trough garden.

Microbiota decussata (Siberian cypress)

For a design requiring a low juniper-like spreading groundcover, this species is the perfect choice. Unlike its juniper look-alikes, Siberian cypress does not require full sun. It favors cool conditions and demands good drainage but tolerates a wide range of soils. This conifer grows less than 12 in. (30 cm) tall with a spread of 6 to 12 ft. (1.8 to 3.6 m). The soft, fine-textured, lacy leaves are in flat sprays that arch over with drooping tips. The foliage is pale green in summer and bronze to purple in winter. Siberian cypress is excellent as a foundation plant or on windy slopes. It is available and deserving of much wider use.

Picea and *Pinus* (spruce and pine)

Pines and spruces (and firs for that matter) are known to grow well only in full sun conditions. However for the gardener hankering to have a spruce in part shade conditions the best choice would be a selection of *Picea orientalis* (oriental spruce). The soft, glossy, dark green needles are shorter than those of any other spruce, and the pollen-bearing

Left: *Microbiota decussata* with Dale Chihuly's *Opaque Float with Gold Leaf and Green Lines* 1955.

Right: A dwarf selection of *Picea orientalis* growing in shade.

cones that appear in the spring are bright red. Many dwarf cushion-shaped cultivars of oriental spruce are worth trying including 'Barnes' (see photo), 'Bergman's Gem', 'Connecticut Turnpike', and 'Nana'.

Taxus baccata and
T. baccata 'Fastigiata'

Taxus (yew)

Taxus includes three species native to North America and one to England, plus hybrids between the species. Yews can be shrubs or trees. They tolerate considerable shade and most soils provided they are well drained. Many selections from these species are used in public landscaping and in both estate and home gardens. They accept trimming and shaping into hedges or topiaries and tolerate urban pollution. Available selections vary from low and wide-spreading to tall and columnar. Although the foliage is poisonous to livestock, most gardeners are familiar with the special fondness of white-tailed deer for garden yews.

Thuja (arborvitae)

Generally available, popular, and very widely used for ornamental purposes, *Thuja occidentalis* (eastern arborvitae) is the species most commonly meant when people speak of arborvitaes. It prefers deep, moist, and humusy soil. The aromatic foliage is displayed in flat sprays.

Although this species does best in full sun, it is considered somewhat shade-tolerant.

There are loads of cultivars, some nearly indistinguishable from each other. For use in mixed borders shrub-sized cultivars include 'Berkmanii' with yellow foliage, the rounded and dense 'Boothii', 'Globosa' with deep green foliage, and the soft yellow 'Golden Globe' (see photo). The extremely slow-growing and commonly available 'Hetz Midget' turns bronze-purple in winter.

Best choices for landscape-sized trees are 'Degroot's Spire' (see photo), which is narrow and tightly branched, and 'Smaragd' (see photo), which grows rapidly but stays compact, narrow and upright. The latter is often listed as 'Emerald Green' because it is considered by many to be the best green among the arborvitaes. It is also good for hedging and is unaffected by snow loads if trained to a single leader.

Superlative for knot gardens is the slow-growing ball 'Tiny Tim' (see photo). Gardeners in suburban areas are well aware of the fondness of deer for this species.

The west coast native *Thuja plicata* (giant arborvitae, western redcedar) is an adaptable conifer that will grow in most soil conditions where dryness is not prolonged. It is a very handsome tree for the home landscape with its luxuriant wide-sweeping boughs. It responds well to pruning and can be trained into a lush hedge. It has been ob-

Thuja occidentalis 'Hetz Midget'

served that deer do not rush to browse on it the way they do toward eastern arborvitae (*T. occidentalis*).

For specimens and screening 'Atrovirens' is a good choice; it is narrow and pyramidal to 30 to 45 ft. (9 to 14 m), has glossy dark green foliage all year, tolerates wet soil, and takes considerable shade. 'Zebrina' has stunning creamy yellow zebra-stripe variegation (see photo).

For an "instant" tree choose *Thuja* 'Green Giant', a hybrid that grows 3 to 5 ft. (0.9 to 1.5 m) a year, reaching 60 ft. (18 m) tall by 20 ft. (6 m) wide; it displays glossy dark green foliage in all seasons.

Thujopsis dolabrata (hiba arborvitae)

Thujopsis dolabrata is another conifer that grows best in an area of partial shade, shelter, and cool dampness. It tolerates cold winters and a wide range of soils. Slow-growing, dense, and pyramidal, it ranges in size from a shrub to a tree 30 to 50 ft. (9 to 15 m) tall. The glossy deep green scalelike leaves have distinctive white markings underneath. There are dwarf, gold, and variegated forms.

Tsuga (hemlock)—A Cautionary Note

Any discussion of conifers for shade involves finding substitutes for *Tsuga canadensis*, a North American native which has been the classic first choice for moist woodland conditions. This most graceful of

Thujopsis dolabrata

conifers with its soft, fine-textured foliage, tolerance of the shade of the forest understory, and acceptance of shaping into elegant hedges, has sadly been threatened in recent years by the relentless march of an insect pest, the woolly adelgid (*Adelges tsugae*).

An infestation is easy to recognize; the egg sacs of these insects look like bits of cotton clinging to the undersides of the needles. Recent climate changes with warmer winters have accelerated the problem, which causes the eventual death of the tree. A nontoxic dormant oil spray can control the infestation but for the homeowner with mature specimens this is often not practical. It is no longer recommended that the species be planted. Nevertheless, dwarf selections of hemlock make beautiful additions to the shady border and can be easily observed for the pest and sprayed when needed without calling in arborists.

Cultivars of hemlock that will add polish to the shady border include 'Bennett', a slow-growing dwarf that becomes a spreading mound 2 ft. (0.6 m) tall by 4 ft. (1.2 m) wide in 10 years and has pendulous branch tips, and 'Cole's Prostrate', which will be a bit flatter and is nice for vest pocket or shady rock gardens (see photo). Also slow-growing are 'Gentsch White', a white-tipped selection, and 'Everitt's Golden', which displays golden-yellow foliage early in the season. 'Little Joe' is ideal for a shady trough garden or bonsai.

Opposite, top: A pendulous *Tsuga canadensis* in a shady spot.

Opposite, bottom: *Tsuga canadensis* 'Gentsch White'

Larger Landscapes

ALTHOUGH MOST GARDENERS and designers are concerned primarily with the many ways conifers can be used *within* a garden rather than in the wider landscape, there are doubtless others with larger properties who want to plant specimen trees, or perhaps new homeowners who have space for one large tree in a sunny spot in their bare yard. Here are some suggestions.

Abies concolor (concolor fir)

One of the most adaptable of the firs, concolor fir tolerates hot summers better than expected for a fir native to the Rocky Mountains. The

Opposite: Serbian spruces (*Picea omorika*) in the larger borrowed landscape.

Left: *Abies concolor*

dense, pyramidal tree grows 8 to 12 in. (20 to 30 cm) per year, reaching 50 ft. (15 m) tall by 20 ft. (6 m) wide. The fragrant needles are bluish on both sides. Concolor fir is an excellent choice for the larger landscape where a blue pyramidal tree is desired. It remains far more attractive over its longer life span than *Picea pungens* (Colorado spruce) and is softer to the touch. 'Candicans', one of the bluest forms, reaches 40 ft. (12 m) tall (see photo).

Araucaria araucana (monkey-puzzle tree)

Native to Chile where it can reach 100 ft. (30 m) tall, monkey-puzzle tree seldom exceeds 30 ft. (9 m) in cultivation. The species dates back to the dinosaurs. It is very slow growing in youth with a single very straight stem and whorled branches. With age the top becomes dome shaped. The leaves are wickedly sharp. This conifer is grown as a landscape tree in the Pacific Northwest and in California and is frequently seen in the United Kingdom. It is definitely for the gardener who wants something unusual.

Cedrus atlantica 'Glauca' (Atlas cedar)

Pyramidal only in youth, this tree becomes wide-spreading with maturity to 60 ft. (18 m) tall by 40 ft. (12 m) wide. Like other cedars, it

Opposite: A mature *Araucaria araucana*.

Below: *Cedrus atlantica*

tolerates heat, drought, and some salt. It is not always attractive in youth, but in 20 years' time it becomes an imposing and picturesque silvery specimen in the larger landscape. This tree will survive our unrelenting global climate change.

Chamaecyparis nootkatensis 'Pendula' (Alaska-cedar)

Alaska-cedar is another Pacific Northwest native. The tree reaches 150 ft. (46 m) tall in the wild and can live 2000 years. It has a weeping

Chamaecyparis nootkatensis

habit with the secondary branchlets draped toward the ground from the principal branches (see photo).

Cryptomeria japonica (Japanese-cedar)

Cryptomerias are some of the oldest and largest living trees of Japan where they can grow to 160 ft. (49 m) tall. Many dwarf forms of the species are recommended elsewhere in this book, but 'Yoshino' (see photo) is for the larger landscape; valued for its graceful habit, shade

Cryptomeria japonica
'Rein's Dense Jade'

Opposite: *Metasequoia glyptostroboides* reveals its architecture in winter.

tolerance, and beautiful rich green foliage, this cultivar grows to 20 ft. (6 m) tall by 8 ft. (2.5 m) wide. Another choice pick is the formal-looking 'Rein's Dense Jade'; its jade-green needles turn bronze in winter.

Juniperus virginiana (eastern red-cedar)

The common name is deceiving, as this species is not a true cedar. Native to the eastern United States, it occupies a wide natural range and is one of the most adaptable of conifers. It normally grows in rocky areas and is found on hillsides, in abandoned fields, along roadsides, or in any dry, sunny situation. The tree grows slowly to 20 to 50 ft. (6 to 15 m) tall. It tolerates extremes of heat, drought, wind, cold, and poor soil, in fact, any condition except heavy shade and very wet sites. Large old specimens have a fluted trunk and in the wild display considerable variability from broadly conical to columnar. The foliage bronzes in the winter. Eastern red-cedar is a dioecious conifer meaning that pollen-bearing cones and seed-bearing cones (these are the juniper berries) are produced on separate trees.

Among the garden-worthy cultivars are 'Canaertii', with year-round dark green foliage and abundant blue "berries," and 'Corcorcor' (synonym 'Emerald Sentinel'), a fast-growing, sturdy, dependable conifer reaching 25 to 30 ft. (8 to 9 m), also with rich green foliage year-round (see photo).

Metasequoia glyptostroboides (dawn redwood)

Dawn redwood was thought to be extinct until found in China in 1941 and seeds collected by the Arnold Arboretum in 1948 were distributed widely. It is vigorous and strong-growing up to 4 ft. (1.2 m) per year, reaching 40 to 50 ft. (12 to 15 m) in less than 20 years. This broad and conical, very orderly and uniform tree has a sharply pointed top on a central single stem. It is deciduous with fall color that changes from a yellow-brown to pink, even apricot, then a copper-brown. The winter habit is very distinctive. Dawn redwood tolerates very wet, even boggy soil for part of the year but accepts dry sites once established. It is immune to pollution and urban conditions. The trunk becomes buttressed and irregularly fluted.

Picea abies (Norway spruce)

Norway spruce is the most common spruce in Europe and the most widely used horticultural spruce in North America for reforestation. It can reach 100 ft. (30 m) tall by 40 ft. (12 m) wide in cultivation. It is a wide pyramidal tree with pendulous secondary branches. This spruce is popular because it is tolerant of a wide range of conditions, grows fast, up to 2 ft. (0.6 m) a year, and is widely available.

Picea orientalis (oriental spruce)

This beautifully shaped pyramidal tree reaches 60 ft. (18 m) tall by 20 ft. (6 m) wide. It is densely branched with graceful, very dark green foliage that is maintained to the ground. The needles are short and soft. Oriental spruce is highly recommended and superior to the ubiquitous Norway spruce.

Left: *Picea abies*

Right: *Picea orientalis* 'Aureospicata'

Pinus strobus (eastern white pine)

The tallest tree native to eastern North America, this pine is very adaptable and grows 1 to 3 ft. (0.3 to 0.9 m) per year. It is pyramidal when young, and open and spreading with age, often becoming flat-topped and irregular. But make note that it is very sensitive to salt and air pollution. This fact is apparently unknown or ignored by developers who routinely plant a row of white pines all along the edge of a subdivision. Because the species is readily damaged by ice and heavy wet snow, the cultivar 'Fastigiata' is much preferred; the branching angles of the cultivar make it less subject to splitting.

Pinus strobus 'Fastigiata'

Pseudotsuga menziesii (Douglas-fir)

Not a fir at all, this conifer is another Pacific Northwest native that can get huge and be very long-lived. It is tough and adaptable. In the landscape it will grow 40 to 80 ft. (12 to 24 m) tall. 'Graceful Grace' is a fast-growing weeping selection with long blue-green needles and an irregular upright leader.

Pseudotsuga menziesii

Sequoiadendron giganteum (giant sequoia)

In its native stands in California, giant sequoia is the largest tree on earth in terms of mass, but in cultivation it is likely to reach about 60 ft. (18 m) tall. When grown in the open as a garden specimen, its branches are retained to the ground. The thick bark is a rich red-brown. This species is widely planted through Europe and is espe-

Sequoiadendron giganteum

cially popular in Great Britain and Germany but strangely underused in the United States.

Taxodium distichum (bald-cypress)

In cultivation bald-cypress will likely reach 50 ft. (15 m) at maturity. It is carefree after it is established. Of all trees it has probably the greatest known tolerance for flooding; some specimens stand in water for half of the growing season. It is a tough and adaptable species. The foliage is deciduous, turning russet or soft brown in autumn (see photo).

Thuja plicata (giant arborvitae, western red-cedar)

Although a giant native of the Pacific Northwest, this species is very adaptable to the eastern United States and should be more widely planted. In cultivation the tree can reach 50 to 70 ft. (15 to 21 m) tall (see photo). It has been observed that deer do not rush to browse on it the way they do towards the eastern arborvitae (*Thuja occidentalis*). 'Zebrina', named for its green and gold striped foliage, reaches over 16 ft. (4.9 m) tall in the first 10 years.

Opposite: *Thuja plicata* 'Zebrina'

Asian-style Gardens

MANY OF US ARE ATTRACTED to Asian gardens because they are so tranquil—places for quiet contemplation where the plantings show restraint and simplicity. Usually the botanical diversity of these gardens is not sizable, although typically more than two-thirds of the plants are evergreen. And among those evergreens, many are conifers.

The Chinese have one of the oldest continuous traditions of garden design. The surrounding landscape of mountains and lakes provides inspiration for their gardens. For centuries the use of rocks and pools together with plants has been central in their design. Chinese gardens exhibit much symbolism of order and harmony and are places to mediate on the unity of nature. Pathways are typically irregular to slow the visitor and permit closer contact with the plants. Plants are carefully chosen for their forms and meaning. Pines are always present. Herbaceous plants commonly used are chrysanthemums, tree peonies, and lotus, each rich with symbolism.

The traditions of Japanese gardens evolved from the Chinese style. Gardens in Japan are meant to represent the greater landscape in miniature: a paring down of the natural world to its essential elements. It is a serene and harmonious naturalistic landscape, often containing islands and waterfalls. Most Japanese gardens will have a stone basin water feature. Flowering plants are typically absent or are used sparingly since they express impermanence and fleeting beauty; conifers and evergreen trees and shrubs are planted to represent eternal beauty. In Japan, age is strongly revered, and gardens include young pine trees that are often pruned and trained to give the illusion of age. Often the "lakes" and "streams" in Japanese gardens are represented by gravel. Specific guiding principles exist for the placement of rocks, which are considered living things, and the raking of gravel. Sometimes a cottage for the tea ceremony is part of the garden. Even though it all looks very natural to the visitor, a Japanese garden is a very carefully controlled landscape and is far from "natural."

Japanese maple (*Acer palmatum*) and Japanese camellia (*Camellia japonica*) along with many species of bamboo and flowering cherries are always included in a Japanese garden. Often azaleas (*Rhododen-*

Opposite: View of a Chinese-style garden. The carefully contoured conifers harmonize with the gentle slope of the hill.

Below: Entrance to a Chinese-style garden. Note how carefully the pine is framed by the entrance.

Opposite, top: Entrance to a Japanese-style garden. The sedums and sumac are a giveaway that this is a westernized version of Japanese style.

Opposite, bottom: Green is the dominant color in Asian gardens; floral color usually appears, if at all, in brief seasonal bursts.

dron) and Japanese iris (*Iris ensata*) provide early spring color. The predominant groundcover is frequently moss. It is not unusual to restrict the number of different kinds of plants used in a single garden. In a Japanese garden nothing is symmetrical: the rocks and trees are always gently skewed, no path is straight. Narrow paths force the visitor to slow down and notice the plants at their feet.

Conifers are rarely permitted to grow untouched in a Japanese garden, so pruning is an essential skill for anyone wanting a Japanese-style garden. Trees are trained to look like they have been present and weathered for centuries by nature with rugged S-shaped trunks and cascading branches. Copper wire, raffia, bamboo stakes, and pruning are used to train plants, and often the interior of a plant is cut away to expose the inner trunk and main branches. The outer branches are then layered into cloud-shapes. Other specimens might be layered out horizontally. Sometimes rocks are fastened to larger branches to pull them down by gravity.

Opposite, top: Tailored plants play an important part in the overall design of all Asian gardens.

Opposite, bottom: The size of conifers can be restricted to suit the scale of the garden. Foliage is pruned each year to control growth.

Whether it is possible to create a truly "Chinese" or "Japanese" garden in a western context is open to debate. What is undeniable is that many elements of Asian gardens appeal strongly to western sensibilities and can be used to great effect, even if their authenticity is questionable.

CONIFER SPECIES REGULARLY USED IN ASIAN GARDEN DESIGNS

- *Chamaecyparis obtusa* (hinoki false cypress): Slow-growing with rich green year-round foliage.
- *Chamaecyparis pisifera* (sawara-cypress): Excellent, develops compact form.
- *Cryptomeria japonica* (Japanese-cedar): Graceful habit, shade tolerant, beautiful foliage.
- *Ginkgo biloba* (maidenhair tree): Distinctive leaves turn bright gold in autumn.
- *Juniperus chinensis* 'Kaizuka' (Chinese juniper): Makes a good specimen plant as it needs no pruning.
- *Juniperus procumbens* 'Nana' (garden juniper): Ideal for growing over a low wall.
- *Pinus densiflora* (Japanese red pine): Valued for its flaking orangish bark.
- *Pinus parviflora* (Japanese white pine): Crooked, picturesque trunk.
- *Pinus thunbergii* (Japanese black pine): Perhaps the most important of Japanese pines.
- *Pseudolarix amabilis* (golden-larch): Dazzling orangish foliage in fall.
- *Sciadopitys verticillata* (Japanese umbrella-pine): Appreciated for its natural balanced habit and luxuriant foliage.
- *Taxus cuspidata* (Japanese yew): Hardy, fast-growing, the easiest yew to cultivate.
- *Thujopsis dolabrata* (hiba arborvitae): Bright green leaves with distinctive white markings underneath.
- *Torreya nucifera* (Japanese torreya): Plumlike seed cones mature to pale purple.

Opposite, top: Plants are often layered horizontally with bamboo stakes—a time-consuming and skill-demanding practice.

Opposite, bottom: A dry garden is intended to create the image of islands and water through the use of sand, stone and sparse plantings. Patterns raked into the gravel represent waves or ripples of water.

Above: Waterfalls are often found in Japanese gardens, here flowing through trained pines.

Opposite, top: Azaleas
are a common source of
ephemeral spring color
in Japanese gardens.

Opposite, bottom:
A cascading yew in a
Japanese-style garden.

Bonsai

BONSAI IS THE ART OF GROWING DWARF TREES in shallow pots. The practice originated in China more than a thousand years ago and made its way to Japan before 1200. It has slowly acquired a distinctively Japanese style.

Plants are meticulously trained to create miniature models of the natural growth patterns of mature plants growing in nature. This is done first by pruning the plants so they remain small, and then forcing them into stylized shapes with copper wire to create the appearance of great age.

Bonsai trees are grown in shallow containers and the roots are periodically pruned to restrict growth. It can take years to achieve the desired style. There exist bonsai plants that are documented to be over 400 years old.

Called a living art form, bonsai can involve a lifetime of study. The tree species is only the beginning; equally important are the pot, the soil, and the shape and style of the training. The styles of the resulting bonsai trees have names like Informal Upright; Formal Upright, Root-over-rock, Semi-cascade, and Cascade. It is advisable for a beginner to join a bonsai club or society.

Opposite: The term "sharimiki" refers to a tree struck by lightning, resulting in the bark or part of the trunk being stripped off. In this 34-year-old *Juniperus procumbens* 'Nana' (common juniper), the area was bleached to simulate the condition.

231

The bonsai display at the Montreal Botanical Garden, Canada includes a 240-year-old *Juniperus communis* (common juniper).

Right: Bonsai are often displayed at eye level against a fence or painted wall. Here is a 350-year-old *Pinus parviflora* (Japanese white pine).

CHOICE CONIFERS FOR BONSAI

- *Cedrus atlantica* 'Glauca' (Atlas cedar): Develops dense, twiggy silver-blue foliage.
- *Chamaecyparis obtusa* (hinoki false cypress): Many slow-growing cultivars.
- *Chamaecyparis pisifera* (sawara-cypress): Excellent choice, develops compact form.
- *Cryptomeria japonica* (Japanese-cedar): Dwarf varieties can be trained into dense growth patterns.
- *Ginkgo biloba* (maidenhair tree): Unique leaves pale green in spring and brilliant gold in autumn.
- *Juniperus chinensis* (Chinese juniper): Nice reddish bark, countless cultivars.
- *Juniperus communis* (common juniper): Not easy, but can produce superb bonsai.
- *Juniperus horizontalis* (prostrate juniper): Good material for bonsai.
- *Juniperus procumbens* (garden juniper): Excellent plant, especially 'Nana'; good choice for first attempts.
- *Larix decidua* (European larch): Deciduous with golden fall color, cones in proportion to bonsai.
- *Larix kaempferi* (Japanese larch): Deciduous, a favorite.
- *Pinus parviflora* (Japanese white pine): A classic plant for bonsai, very long lived.
- *Pinus sylvestris* (Scots pine): Hardy, easy to train, flaky red-brown bark.
- *Pinus thunbergii* (Japanese black pine): Especially popular in Japan.
- *Taxus baccata* (English yew): Extremely good choice, easy to train, glossy black-green needles.

Shaping branches and trunks with copper wire is the most used and most important technique in bonsai training, allowing the bonsai designer to create the desired general form and make detailed branch placements.

Above, right: In this style of bonsai the height of the first branch up from the base of the trunk should be one-third of the total height of the tree, as it is for this *Chamaecyparis obtusa* (hinoki false cypress).

Right: A strong surface root structure and trunk buttress help give a mature appearance to a 37-year-old *Pinus sylvestris* (Scots pine).

Ideally the depth of the pot should be approximately the same as the diameter of the base of the trunk. This *Chamaecyparis obtusa* is 134 years old.

Left: Space between branches is important, and allows light into the branches. Shown here is a 154-year-old *Pinus parviflora* (Japanese white pine).

Opposite, top: In bonsai, *jin* refers to a dead branch that has lost its bark or had it removed. *Jin* plays a very important part in the final appearance of a bonsai because it creates a small but significant detail in the illusion of maturity. Occasionally, as in this *Juniperus chinensis* 'San Jose' (Chinese juniper), branches are painted to appear dead.

Opposite, bottom: The winter protection of very old bonsai, such as this 350-year-old *Pinus parviflora* (Japanese white pine), can sometimes be quite elaborate.

Railway Gardens

MANY MEN OF A CERTAIN AGE had model Lionel trains in their youth set up on a table in the basement or remember their being arranged annually under the family holiday tree. Today, however, for many persons of all ages, installing, operating, and maintaining an outdoor garden railroad (or "railway") is a serious, and expensive, hobby.

Garden railroading is a combination of installing model railroads out of doors and establishing miniature landscapes including bridges, crossings, and villages for the locomotive to chug its way through. The buildings, often made by the hobbyist, are in scale with the railway cars. In the best installations the plants, representing the trees and shrubs in the countryside the train travels through, are permanent plantings and are in scale with the entire display. Sometimes tunnels through "mountains" and rock formations with waterfalls are part of the display. Often the trains have audio on-board and sound like real trains.

Opposite: Dwarf arborvitaes (*Thuja*) flank a rustic bridge.

Below: The conifers here are but one element in a richly planted miniature landscape.

The "architecture" here gives the scene an alpine feel.

The display of model railroads began initially as a business practice to promote railroad travel to the general public during the building of the national railroads in the middle of the nineteenth century. It soon developed as a hobby, initially in Germany, spreading from there to Britain and eventually to North America. Along the line many differences had to be worked out related to the "scale" of the train cars and tracks.

If anything, garden railways are more popular than ever. There are a half dozen magazines and many newsletters published for "railroaders." Most have an advice column by knowledgeable horticulturists with recommendations for suitable plants. There are over a hundred garden railway clubs throughout the country which serve as a focus for social gatherings and the exchange of ideas.

Many public arboretums and botanic gardens have installed permanent railway displays as a way to attract families to their grounds and introduce them to their many additional educational and recreational benefits. The spectacular display at the Morris Arboretum of the University of Pennsylvania, for instance, annually changes the theme of the highly detailed buildings along the course of their many trains. In England near London at Beaconsfield, Buckinghamshire, at Bekonscot Model Village is one of the oldest and largest garden railways in the world with a model village set in the 1930s.

Conifer Selections for the Garden Railway

Some railroaders develop a parallel interest in finding just the exact plants for their concept (not to mention their growing conditions) and even employ bonsai techniques on their plants to insure the appearance of aged forest trees. Dwarf, even miniature slow-growing cultivars are obviously excellent choices. It is important that plants have slow annual growth to reduce maintenance. Small-scaled herbaceous plants, especially grasses, mosses, and tiny-leaved creeping herbs are used to add texture and realism to the landscapes.

Abies concolor 'Compacta' (concolor fir): irregularly rounded and slow-growing, reaches 2 ft. (0.6 m) tall after many years.

Abies koreana 'Cis' (Korean fir): dwarf and bushy with rich dark green needles, grows 1 in. (2.5 cm) a year.

Abies koreana 'Silberkugel' (Korean fir): dwarf and rounded, displaying bright green needles with silver undersides.

Abies pinsapo 'Horstmann' (Spanish fir): an attractive low-spreading compact dwarf with stiff blue foliage, grows 4 in. (10 cm) a year.

Cedrus deodara 'Feelin' Blue' (deodar cedar): a dwarf spreading form with gray-blue foliage, reaches 1 ft. (0.3 m) tall by 3 ft. (0.9 m) wide in 10 years (see photo).

Cedrus libani 'Green Prince' (cedar of Lebanon): slow-growing 1 in. (2.5 cm) a year, deep green dwarf that becomes an open-branched pyramid giving the appearance of great age, excellent choice.

Chamaecyparis lawsoniana 'Green Globe' (Lawson false cypress): a

Left: *Abies koreana* 'Cis'

Right: *Abies koreana* 'Silberkugel'

dense rounded compact dwarf eventually reaching 1 to 2 ft. (0.3 to 0.6 m) tall, perfect.

Chamaecyparis obtusa 'Green Cushion' (hinoki false cypress): a very dwarf bun.

Chamaecyparis obtusa 'Jean Iseli' (hinoki false cypress): a miniature mound with deep green compact foliage.

Chamaecyparis obtusa 'Little Marky' (hinoki false cypress): a dense pyramidal dwarf with chartreuse-yellow foliage, reaches 30 in. (75 cm) tall in 15 years.

Chamaecyparis obtusa 'Minima' (hinoki false cypress): a very slow growing tight bun, can take 10 years to reach 6 in. (15 cm) tall.

Chamaecyparis pisifera 'Boulevard' (sawara-cypress): soft silver-blue juvenile foliage, becomes purple-tinged in winter, withstands heavy pruning to desired shape.

Chamaecyparis pisifera 'White Pygmy' (sawara-cypress): white feathery new growth with green within, forms a flat globe only 3 ft. (0.9 m) tall by 12 in. (30.5 cm) wide after 10 years.

Cryptomeria japonica 'Koshyi' (Japanese-cedar): spreading habit, reaching 6 in. (15 cm) tall by 20 in. (50 cm) wide in 20 years, pale green foliage, needs protection from afternoon sun and winter wind.

Ginkgo biloba 'Chi-chi' (maidenhair tree): a dwarf, dense, multi-stemmed habit, reaches 4 ft (1.2 m) tall in 10 years, male.

Juniperus communis 'Compressa' (common juniper): a slow-growing narrow upright dwarf, cone-shaped without shearing, fine-textured silvery blue-green foliage, grows 2 in. (5 cm) a year to 3 ft. (0.9 m) tall (see photo).

Juniperus communis 'Green Carpet' (common juniper): a slow-

Left: *Chamaecyparis obtusa* 'Little Marky'

Right: *Chamaecyparis obtusa* 'Minima'

growing prostrate mat of bright green juvenile foliage, hardy and adaptable.

Juniperus horizontalis 'Mother Lode' (prostrate juniper): brilliant gold foliage in summer turning to shades of deep gold and salmon-orange with green overtones in winter, provide full sun with good drainage, very slow-growing (see photo).

Juniperus horizontalis 'Prince of Wales' (prostrate juniper): low-growing and broad-spreading, dense, soft-appearing bright green foliage with a hint of blue, 4 to 6 in. (10 to 15 cm) tall.

Juniperus procumbens 'Nana' (garden juniper): slowly forms a compact spreading mat less than 1 ft. (0.3 m) tall, prickly blue-green foliage in all seasons, an excellent selection for shaping into a tree shape (see photo).

Larix kaempferi 'Wolterdingen' (Japanese larch): dwarf, slow-grow-

Top, left: *Chamaecyparis pisifera* 'Boulevard'

Top, right: *Chamaecyparis pisifera* 'White Pygmy'

Bottom, left: *Cryptomeria japonica* 'Koshyi'

Bottom, right: *Larix kaempferi* 'Wolterdingen'

ing, irregular conical growth reaches 20 in. (50 cm) tall by 24 in. (60 cm) wide in 10 years, deciduous blue-green foliage.

Picea abies 'Clanbrassiliana' (Norway spruce); dense and flat-topped, wider than tall, only 3 ft (0.9 cm) tall after decades.

Picea abies 'Little Gem' (Norway spruce): a tight flat dome of dense branches with small light green soft needles, grows 1 to 2 in. (2.5 to 5 cm) a year.

Picea abies 'Pygmaea' (Norway spruce): an extremely slow-growing, compact shrub becoming broad and dome-shaped, reaches 18 in. (46 cm) tall after many years, outstanding.

Picea glauca 'Alberta Globe' (white spruce): slow-growing, neat, and rounded with dense short needles, reaches 24 in. (60 cm) tall by 20 in. (50 cm) wide in 10 years.

Picea glauca 'Blue Planet' (white spruce): a dense flat globe with short blue needles, slow-growing.

Picea glauca 'Cecilia' (white spruce): compact with short glossy dense silver-blue needles, flat and spreading. slow-growing.

Picea glauca 'Conica' (dwarf Alberta white spruce): compact and slow-growing with dense needles, becomes 3 to 4 ft. (0.9 to 1.2 m) tall by 18 in. (46 cm) wide in 10 to 15 years, best in a cool location with some shade and good air circulation, needs protection from hot and cold winds, reflected sunlight and heat from walls.

Picea glauca 'Jean's Dilly' (white spruce): slower growing than 'Conica', even more tailored and darker green.

Picea glauca 'Laurin' (white spruce): a slow-growing cone to 10 in. (25 cm) tall.

Picea abies 'Little Gem'

Picea glauca 'Little Globe' (white spruce): rounded dense habit, growing only 1 in. (2.5 cm) a year.

Picea glauca 'Pixie' (white spruce): upright narrow cone with dark green needles, slow-growing, reaches 12 in. (30 cm) tall in 10 years, possibly the favorite of railway enthusiasts (see photo).

Picea glauca 'Pixie Dust' (white spruce): dense and compact, emerging bud growth is yellow, reaches 16 in. (40 cm) tall in 10 years.

Picea omorika 'Nana' (Serbian spruce): a broadly conical shrub with two-toned needles, eventually becomes pyramidal, reaches 3 ft. (0.9 cm) tall in 10 years.

Picea omorika 'Pimoko' (Serbian spruce): short blue-green needles with silver undersides on short branches, smaller than 'Nana'.

Picea omorika 'Zuckerhut' (Serbian spruce): a dwarf cone with dense green needles.

Picea orientalis 'Tom Thumb' (oriental spruce): a dwarf and globose with golden new foliage.

Pinus aristata 'Sherwood Compact' (bristlecone pine): very slow growing, not tolerant of heat.

Left: *Picea glauca* 'Pixie Dust'

Right: *Pinus aristata* 'Sherwood Compact'

Pinus cembra 'Blue Mound': low and mounding reaching 3 ft. (0.9 m) tall by 2 ft. (0.6 m) wide in 16 years.

Pinus cembra 'Nana' (Swiss stone pine): a slow-growing pyramidal dwarf for small gardens, reaches 24 in. (60 cm) tall in 10 years.

Pinus leucodermis 'Compact Gem' (Bosnian pine): a slow-growing dwarf with a slender, dense, compact, conical shape, tolerant of drought and salt (see photo).

Pinus leucodermis 'Smidtii' (Bosnian pine): a dense compact mound, grows 1 in. (2.5 cm) a year.

Pinus mugo 'Gnom' (mugo pine): compact, with deep jade-green foliage that grows in a dense, globular mound.

Pinus mugo 'Jakobsen' (mugo pine): a flat and spreading selection with thick, somewhat contorted dark green needles, grows 3 in (7.5 cm) a year.

Pinus mugo 'Mitsch Mini' (mugo pine): one of the best bun-shaped mugos but very slow-growing at 1 in. (2.5 cm) a year, short dark green twisted needles year-round, very salt-tolerant.

Pinus mugo 'Mops' (mugo pine): formal, compact, and globose, reaches 3 ft. (0.9 m) tall, growing about 2 in. (5 cm) a year, resinous bright green needles yellow a bit in winter.

Pinus mugo 'Sherwood Compact' (mugo pine): dwarf, compact, and globe-shaped, growing only 1 to 2 in. (2.5 to 5 cm) a year, dark green year-round, a superb choice.

Pinus mugo 'Slowmound' (mugo pine): a dwarf uniform flat carpet of upward-facing shoots, slow-growing.

Left: *Pinus leucodermis* 'Smidtii'

Right: *Pinus mugo* 'Jakobsen'

Pinus parviflora 'Adcock's Dwarf' (Japanese white pine): a dense, slow-growing globose form with short gray-green needles clustered at the branch tips, reaches 3 to 4 ft. (0.9 to 1.2 m) tall after 25 years.

Pinus parviflora 'Bergman' (Japanese white pine): grows 2 in. (5 cm) a year to produce a broadly conical plant with twisted blue-green needles, pollen-bearing cones are bright red in the spring.

Pinus parviflora 'Glauca Nana' (Japanese white pine): extremely slow-growing with an open habit, eventually becomes a flat-topped globe with short twisted, blue needles.

Pinus parviflora 'Goldilocks' (Japanese white pine): a small cushion with bright gold leaves that burn in full sun.

Pinus strobus 'Blue Shag' (eastern white pine): slow-growing, 4 in. (10 cm) a year, with a dense rounded habit and silver-blue needles.

Pinus strobus 'Minuta' (eastern white pine): a low-growing compact bun with short blue-green needles, reaching 5 ft. (1.5 m) tall after 20 years.

Top, left: *Pinus mugo* 'Slowmound'

Bottom, left: *Pinus strobus* 'Minuta'

Below: *Pinus parviflora* 'Goldilocks'

Pinus strobus 'Sea Urchin' (eastern white pine): thin but dense blue needles on a low mounded plant that grows only 2 in. (5 cm) a year to 3 to 4 ft. (0.9 to 1.2 m) tall and wide (see photo).

Pinus sylvestris 'Watereri' (Scots pine): usually considered a dwarf plant with a globose form, only 8 to 12 in. (20 to 30 cm) tall and wide, but it can grow 4 to 6 in. (10 to 15 cm) a year to 12 ft. (3.6 m) tall, foliage appears blue (see photo).

Pseudotsuga menziesii 'Pumila' (Douglas-fir): a shrub form.

Sequoiadendron giganteum 'Blauer Eichzwerg' (giant sequoia): slow-growing, pyramidal miniature, blue foliage, reaches 3 ft. (0.9 m) tall in 10 years. Ideal.

Sequoiadendron giganteum 'Blauer Eichzwerg'

Taxus ×media 'Beanpole (hybrid yew): a very narrow, 8 in. (20 cm), dense, fastigiated form, slow-growing, female (see photo).

Thuja occidentalis 'Golden Tuffet' (eastern arborvitae): pillow-shaped, golden orange foliage looks braided (see photo).

Thuja occidentalis 'Hetz Midget' (eastern arborvitae): extremely slow-growing, broad, rounded, dense dark green foliage turns bronze-purple in winter, reaches 3 to 4 ft. (0.9 to 1.2 m) tall (see photo).

Thuja occidentalis 'Tiny Tim' (eastern arborvitae): slow-growing ball, reaches 16 in. (40 cm) tall by 12 in. (30 cm) wide in 8 to 10 years.

Thujopsis dolabrata 'Nana' (hiba arborvitae): dwarf, compact, mounded plant slowly reaching 3 ft. (0.9 m) tall, bright green foliage turns olive-green in winter, good for shady spot.

Tsuga canadensis 'Bennett' (eastern hemlock): slow-growing dwarf, spreading mound with pendulous branch tips, dark green foliage, becomes 2 ft. (0.6 m) tall by 4 ft. (1.2 m) wide in 10 years.

Tsuga canadensis 'Cole's Prostrate' (eastern hemlock): slow-growing, mat-forming with branches extending flat along the ground, silver-gray center branches become exposed with maturity, grows 3 ft. (0.9 m) tall in 20 years (see photo).

Tsuga canadensis 'Gentsch White' (eastern hemlock): slow-growing shrub, white-tipped or variegated foliage, benefits from occasional shearing, reaches 2 ft. (0.6 m) tall by 3 ft. (0.9 m) wide.

Tsuga canadensis 'Jeddeloh'; low-spreading and nestlike with pendulous branch tips, similar to 'Bennett'.

Left: *Thuja occidentalis* 'Tiny Tim'

Right: *Tsuga canadensis* 'Gentsch White'

Underused Conifers

THERE ARE TWO SPECIES GROWING in nature and in gardens in the Pacific Northwest that travel well and should be more widely used in other areas of the country: incense-cedar (*Calocedrus decurrens*) and Alaska-cedar (*Chamaecyparis nootkatensis*). And two other species that deserve wider use are suitable for part shade and could substitute for the ubiquitous junipers that do not tolerate anything less than full sun or for dwarf hemlocks: Siberian cypress (*Microbiota decussata*) and Japanese plum-yew (*Cephalotaxus harringtonia*).

Calocedrus decurrens (incense-cedar)

Incense-cedar is native to the mountains from western Oregon south to Northern California but will do just as well in the U.S. Southwest and large portions of the Northeast and Upper South. It is narrow and columnar, reminiscent of the Italian cypress (*Cupressus sempervirens*), and displays lustrous deep green foliage in fanlike branchlets. It carries snow well unlike the eastern arborvitae (*Thuja occidentalis*), which is everywhere, and it also stays green all winter unlike the arborvitae species.

The incense-cedar tree can get very tall in the wild, but in cultivation it will likely grow about a foot (30 cm) a year to 30 to 50 ft. (9 to

Opposite: *Calocedrus decurrens*

Left: *Calocedrus decurrens* 'Aureovariegata' foliage.

Bark of *Calocedrus*.

Opposite, top left: *Cephalotaxus harringtonia* 'Fastigiata'

Opposite, bottom left: *Cephalotaxus harringtonia* 'Fastigiata'

Opposite, top right: *Cephalotaxus harringtonia* 'Korean Gold'

Opposite, bottom right: *Cephalotaxus harringtonia* 'Prostrata'

15 m) tall with a spread of only 8 ft. (2.4 m). The fire-resistant bark is cinnamon red with deep furrowing. Once it is established, the tree is very drought tolerant; in the wild it inhabits areas that receive as little as 15 in. (38 cm) of annual rainfall. It should, however, be sheltered from strong winds. A single specimen lends a formal effect to the garden.

Several cultivars are readily available. 'Aureovariegata' has leaves splashed with yellow and green, and 'Berrima Gold' is a bright gold form that looks deep gold to orange in the winter.

Cephalotaxus harringtonia (Japanese plum-yew)

Yews (*Taxus* spp.) are used widely in public and private gardens as hedges and screening plants, trimmed as topiaries, and for the ubiquitous foundation plantings. However a cousin, the Japanese plum-yew (*Cephalotaxus harringtonia*), is not nearly so familiar. Its cultivars have the same tolerance for shade as the yews but grow slower and require much less maintenance. They are more tolerant of heat and drought and should be utilized in southern gardens. Perhaps the most remarkable difference from yews is that deer do not browse on plum-yew.

Several cultivars are available for home gardens. 'Fastigiata' is slow-growing, narrow and upright, eventually becoming vase-shaped; the foliage radiates around the stem. 'Korean Gold' is similar to 'Fastigiata' except the new growth is bright golden yellow. A low-growing form, 'Prostrata', with its spreading branches, 2 to 3 ft. (0.6 to 0.9 m) high and wide, is useful as a low informal hedge or foundation planting.

Chamaecyparis nootkatensis (Alaska-cedar)

Alaska-cedar is a refined and graceful tree that will lend a distinct character to any yard. Native from southeastern coastal Alaska to northern Oregon, it has a moderate rate of growth and will take many years to reach its mature size of 30 to 40 ft. (9 to 12 m) tall, so there is no need to worry about huge-blue-spruce scenarios. There is an ethereal weeping form called 'Pendula', and a spiky, narrow form called 'Green Arrow'. Either cultivar could be planted singly as a specimen or in a thoughtfully spaced group. Both will appear to float lightly about the ground throughout the year. Alaska-cedar is surprisingly adaptable in cultivation. It does quite well in the U.S. Northeast and, provided it has even supply of moisture, can even cope with the hot summers of the Southeast and Upper Midwest. It needs good drainage.

Opposite: *Chamaecyparis nootkatensis* 'Pendula'

Below: A trio of *Chamaecyparis nootkatensis* 'Green Arrow' make dramatic accents in an island bed with Japanese maples in the distance of a country estate.

Above: *Microbiota
decussata*

Right: *Microbiota decus-
sata* in winter

Microbiota decussata (Siberian cypress)

As its common name suggests, this species is native to eastern Siberia. It is very cold hardy, dense, prostrate, and juniper-like. The plant prefers cool conditions and demands good drainage but tolerates a wide range of soils. Unusual for a conifer, it prefers to grow in high shade, but it will do well in full sun with adequate moisture. Although only topping out at 12 in. (30 cm) high, it can spread 6 to 12 ft. (1.8 to 3.6 m) wide. The soft, fine-textured, lacy leaves are in flat sprays that arch over with drooping tips. The pale green summer foliage turns bronze to purple in winter. Siberian cypress is probably not a good choice for southern gardens.

4

Case Study:

THE
BARRETT GARDEN

Cᴀssᴀɴᴅʀᴀ ᴀɴᴅ Bʀʏᴀɴ Bᴀʀʀᴇᴛᴛ have operated a landscape design and installation business out of their home not far from Eugene, Oregon, for more than 15 years. They are a dynamic pair who are passionate about their profession. Their 2½ acre (1 hectare) personal garden surrounds their home and serves as a resource when they discuss designs with clients. Cassandra hand draws her original designs for each client. Together, the pair take responsibility for all phases of their commissions: design, installation of hardscaping and plants, and maintenance.

I have visited their garden in different seasons and consider it a garden that exemplifies, better than any I have seen, the way well-selected conifers can be imaginatively integrated into complex mixed borders that provide structure and interest throughout the year without excessive maintenance.

Overleaf: Conifers are imaginatively integrated into mixed borders in Cassandra and Bryan Barrett's garden in southern Oregon.

Opposite: The welcoming path to the front garden viewed from the porch in summer.

Below: A slow-growing blue spruce at the moon gate entrance to the back garden repeats the color of the arbor and keeps the structure in scale with the plantings.

Opposite, top: An exceptionally bright container in the back garden complements and contrasts with the garden's plant palette.

Opposite, bottom: Another view of the back garden, with golden oriental arborvitae (*Thuja orientalis* 'Sunlight') in the foreground.

CASSANDRA'S DESIGN PRINCIPLES

◆ *Plan the hardscaping first. As you put in paths, amend soil when necessary, place boulders, install night lighting and irrigation, you are also creating borders.*

◆ *Scale is über important.*

◆ *Pay special attention to the entrance into the garden.*

◆ *Design for views from inside the house. Be sure to use plants that echo colors of the exterior of your home.*

◆ *Pick plants for their fall display and winter color. If the design is not thought out for those seasons, the design will be disappointing.*

◆ *Plant the big things first needed for screening and then begin the intimate space.*

◆ *Choose plants for how they will perform in all seasons: 50 percent for fall and winter, 25 percent for spring, and 25 percent for summer.*

◆ *Use fewer plants and bolder design for a big house on a small lot. Everything has to be in scale.*

◆ *Select conifers that are slow-growing and preferably growing on their own roots.*

◆ *Pick about five plants (deciduous woody, conifer, herbaceous, evergreen) that you repeat throughout your garden to generate design continuity.*

◆ *Include some specimen plants that give pizzazz.*

◆ *Plant the understory densely by using a rhythmic design that repeats throughout the perimeter plantings; mulch gardens are uninspired.*

◆ *Marry the house to the landscape.*

◆ *"Grow to know." The descriptions of newly introduced plants are often inaccurate so don't be afraid to trial a plant in your garden so you can determine where it might best fit into your design.*

◆ *Scout for exceptional garden containers. Pick colors that compliment or contrast with your plant palette.*

◆ *Don't hesitate to work with a plant-oriented landscape designer. A professional can save you.*

The front garden from the house.

The Front Border

The section of garden in front of the Barretts' Arts & Crafts style home will serve as an example to illustrate many of the ideas discussed in the preceding chapters. Since the flow through the present garden seems so natural and the plantings, while complex, strike me as being all of a piece, I asked Cassandra if she would "deconstruct" a portion of the garden and explain in detail both the design principles and the reasons for specific plant selections. The rest of the chapter is her response in her own words.

I have always been drawn to conifers because they are so interesting to look at individually all year, their habits, their new growth, so many different textures; they are indispensable but also functional. They provide screens and are not messy. They drop their needles immediately below. The new growth is so beautiful—larches (Larix), bald-cypress (Taxodium distichum), the candles on pines—every bit as fabulous as seeing the buds swell on a flowering cherry. The conundrum of many designers is that they are not very knowledge-able about the habits and variety of slow-growing conifers and there-fore are timid in their use of conifers.

When designing a frontside garden, I like to design from inside the house as well as outside. To me, the view from the house is as important as the foundation plantings, which are often meant only to frame the house as viewed from the road.

I design a border as if I were decorating a room. First, I decide where the big things go, what needs to be hidden, and what part of the larger space I want to borrow. Only then can I begin to design the more intimate spaces.

I start with the textures, colors, and shapes of the conifers and then work in the other forms—upright, globular, spreading. When I design, I visualize in layers. The views framed by the windows are part of the design process. The area of this planting scheme is only 30 by 100 ft. (9 by 30.5 m).

Upper Story Plantings

In the upper story I'll plant selections that have a medium growth rate. Using taller plants in even limited space actually makes the area look bigger because of the step-down heights within the group plant-ing. The taller plants not only screen what is behind (in this case the township road) but also frame the foreground plantings and, in a larger sense, the house.

Pinus virginiana *'Wate's Golden' (1) was used because it is a fresh green in the summer, but is a school bus yellow from mid-autumn to early summer (October to June). It has a somewhat stiff texture and can be candled to keep it compact. Alternate choices here are* Picea orientalis *'Skylands' or* Cupressus macrocarpa *'Wilma'.*

Chamaecyparis lawsoniana *'Pelt's Blue' (2) is powder blue year-round and has a lacy texture. Other options include* Cupressus gla-bra *'Blue Ice' (shearing necessary) and three selections of* Chamaecy-paris lawsoniana—*'Oregon Blue' (for larger scale area), 'Columnaris Glauca', or 'Pembury Blue'.*

I love the soft and fluffy texture of Cryptomeria japonica *'Elegans' (3) and especially that it turns a smoky plum in the winter. An alter-nate choice is* Chamaecyparis thyoides *'Ericoides'.*

I use Chamaecyparis nootkatensis *'Glauca Pendula' (4) here and elsewhere in the garden because it is very narrow and graceful. Ulti-mately it is the tallest plant in this area. Considering the "borrowed"*

landscape (actually the evolving extension of our garden across the road), there is a natural looking grouping of three of these. Good substitutes are C. lawsoniana *'Dik's Weeping' and 'Wissel's Saguaro' or* Sequoiadendron giganteum *'Pendulum'.*

Chamaecyparis obtusa 'Gracilis' (5) is a favorite. It is easy, available, and has good color all year. I love its fan-shaped foliage.

All these plants have somewhat different habits and textures and some change color through the seasons, but they are very complementary. I think they actually make the space seem larger, even though it is only 32 feet (9.8 m) from the porch steps to the road.

Mid Story Plantings

My primary consideration in mid story plantings is to fill this space on a "human" scale. By that I mean the plants are on eye level and the visitor is going to notice them the most. Here I go back to the analogy of decorating a room. It is in the choice of plants for the mid story that you introduce your style and individual taste whether it be minimalist, formal, cottage, or full of pizzazz. In any case, good

design principles must still be followed. The mid story is the largest mass of plants and it needs to be well thought-out. The mid story also includes conifers for color and texture.

Juniperus communis *'Pencil Point' (2)* was used because it is a taller selection than *'Compressa' (1)* and it is tighter than J. scopulorum *'Skyrocket'*. Thuja orientalis *'Sunlight' (3)* is cone-shaped with vertical sprays of foliage, while Pinus strobus *'Horsford' (4)* displays soft green needles with silvery reflection. I use Chamaecyparis lawsoniana *'Duncanii' (5)* because it keeps its rounded shape without shearing and handles snow well. Abies koreana *'Silberlocke' (6)* is slow-growing with sterling silver curled needles in summer that turn powder blue in winter. The dwarf Pinus contorta var. latifolia *'Chief Joseph' (7)* has striking yellow winter color which ties in with Pinus virginiana *'Wate's Golden' (#1 in the upper story photo)*.

I like to use about five reliable plants in a section that I then repeat elsewhere in the garden. This unifies borders throughout a larger garden even though each border might have a different focus. The plantings might include conifers, broad-leaved evergreens, or larger herba-

Mid story conifer plantings:
1 *Juniperus communis* 'Compressa'; 2 *Juniperus communis* 'Pencil Point'; 3 *Thuja orientalis* 'Sunlight'; 4 *Pinus strobus* 'Horsford'; 5 *Chamaecyparis lawsoniana* 'Duncanii'; 6 *Abies koreana* 'Silberlocke' (hidden in picture); 7 *Pinus contorta* var. *latifolia* 'Chief Joseph'; 8 *Cedrus deodara* 'Devinely Blue'; 9 *Tsuga canadensis* 'Jeddeloh'; 10 *Pinus aristata* 'Sherwood Compact'; 11 *Abies procera* (Glauca Group) 'Nana'; 12 *Cedrus libani* 'Sargentii' (hidden).

Mid story deciduous plants:
A *Physocarpus opulofolius* 'Diabolo' (hidden in photo); B *Corylus avellana* 'Contorta'; C *Hamamelis ´ intermedia* 'Primavera' and 'Diane'; D *Aralia elata* 'Aureovariegata'; E *Mahonia ´ media* 'Charity'; F *Hebe insularis* 'James Stirling'; G *Cercidiphyllum japonicum* 'Rotfuchs'; H *Rhododendron* 'Night Editor'; J *Clematis* 'Jackmanii Superba', 'Betty Corning', or 'Gravetye Beauty'.

ceous plants, but always trying to provide multiseason interest. Some examples are Berberis thunbergii *'Concorde',* Thuja orientalis *'Sunlight',* Picea pungens *'Glauca Globosa',* Mahonia ×media *'Charity',* Cornus sanguinea *'Midwinter Fire',* and Corylus avellana *'Contorta'.*

Tough and very hardy, the burgundy foliage of Physocarpus opulofolius *'Diabolo' (A) is a great contrast in itself, but the pink flowers and lacquer red fruit are a bonus. I cut back the older growth every other spring. I use 'Summer Wine' for tighter areas because of its smaller stature.*

The winter silhouette of Corylus avellana *'Contorta' (B) is without equal and the golden catkins really stand out. Newer cultivars are becoming available with pink catkins and outstanding burgundy foliage.*

Hamamelis ×intermedia *'Primavera' and 'Diane' (C) are indispensible for their yellow fall color and their late winter fragrant flowers. I also love their vase-shaped habits which allow for easy planting around the bases. Again, beware of suckers if your plants are grafted.*

I love the bold-textured variegated foliage and the late summer showy flowers of Aralia elata *'Aureovariegata' (D). It is a real bee magnet. I also like 'Variegata', and I love to use the more elegant 'Silver Umbrella' when space permits. It's dazzling. You must remove root suckers. Still another plant I use here is* Cornus kousa *'Wolf Eyes'.*

Mahonia ×media *'Charity' (E) is planted for the very bold-textured foliage and the fragrant late winter yellow flowers, which are visited by honey bees when they first venture out on warm afternoons. The small blue fruits are gorgeous until they are devoured by cedar wax-wings. Alternate choices are* Osmanthus heterophyllus *'Goshiki' and 'Ogon' or* Elaeagnus ×ebbingei *'Gilt Edge'. Hidden behind the mahonia is a short-statured* Choisya ternata *'Sundance' which I grow because it is evergreen, or rather a lovely bold yellow. Also hidden are* Daphne ×napolitana *and* D. ×houtteana. *I like the waxy surface to the leaf and the green is dark and the yellow a nice primrose.*

Hebe insularis *'James Stirling' (F) has unusual color—bronze— and a very architectural dome-shaped growth habit. It is fine-textured and is echoed by* Carex comans *bronze-leaved (#3 in the understory photo). An alternate,* Cornus sanguinea *'Midwinter Fire', has clean variegated foliage all season, can be a low dense screen, and in winter it absolutely grabs your attention. The effect of the bloom in summer isn't bad either.*

*Although they aren't visible in the photo, I can't have enough tree peonies (*Paeonia suffruticosa*). These are ancient, wonderful long-lived plants. I use the Itoh hybrids for their compact size. Their seed heads and multi-colored fall foliage are sizzling. The huge showy flowers are absolutely spectacular. Also hidden is* Cotinus coggygria *'Velvet Cloak', which I selectively tip back early every spring to shape the crown and grow it for the wonderful burgundy foliage, airy flowers, and variable fall color. Alternative choices includes* C. *'Grace' or* C. coggygria *'Pink Champagne'.*

The heart-shaped leaves of Cercidiphyllum japonicum *'Rotfuchs' (G) are great and I really look forward to the clear yellow-colored leaves in the fall with their delightful candy-cotton fragrance. This is a good choice here in the Pacific Northwest.*

The small leaves and purple flowers of Rhododendron *'Night Editor' (H) are terrific and with its stiff open habit, I can underplant it. Other options are* Rhododendron *PJM hybrids and* Hydrangea serrata *'Tiara'.*

I love to include a clematis here and there in the border, growing upright on a metal teepee. Three favorites are Clematis *'Jackmanii Superba',* C. *'Betty Corning', and* C. *'Gravetye Beauty'.*

Understory Plantings

Many clients don't want this many plants. They are used to a mulch garden with a few plants at arm's length from one another. It reminds me of what the Count told Mozart about one of his compositions: "It's nice but there are too many notes."

Other plants that I like to use in the understory are Andromeda polifolia *'Blue Ice';* Berberis thunbergii *'Concorde';* Crocus sativus *and* C. tommasinianus; Deschampsia cespitosa *'Northern Lights';* Hakonechloa macra *'All Gold', 'Aureola', and 'Variegata';* Helleborus ×hybridus *and especially* H. multifidus *(because of the very finely dissected leaves);* Iris cristata, I. ensata, I. sibirica *tetraploids, and* I. Pacific Coast hybrids; Narcissus *'Jetfire' and 'Tête-à-tête' (both are small and colonize, and their foliage goes away quickly);* Pennisetum orientale *'Karley Rose';* Pulsatilla vulgaris; Paeonia anomala, P. japonica, P. tenuifolia, *and* P. veitchii; *and* Sternbergia lutea.

The Front Border in Winter

The border looks bigger this time of year because of the absence of leaves on the deciduous shrubs and trees and the shapes of the dormant perennials. The bones of the design stand out now. If a design is not cleverly thought-out for its fall and winter appearance the garden will be disappointing. The foundation pattern becomes apparent this time of year. Don't we go to gardens to be enchanted? Unfortunately many borders are blah during these seasons and do not encourage lingering. Now really, doesn't the border look almost as great as it did in the summer season? At this time you are especially aware of the layers but you still do not see our road. Nor is the viewer aware that the border is actually rather narrow for its length. I think it keeps you engaged, perhaps especially this time of year when some

Winter view of the front garden looking toward the road.

Winter view of the front garden looking toward the house. In the right foreground is *Abies koreana* 'Silberlocke', a choice fir that doesn't outgrow its spot. Small, irregular front beds create a natural-looking garden that makes the house one with the landscape. The scale has been kept human sized and in relation to the house, creating the illusion that the garden is bigger than it is.

plants really come to the fore. The winter picture is the blueprint of the design, where one has to start. Now one can see why the plants were picked: layers, textures, colored stems, vibrancy, and even fragrant winter flower.

In the upper story, take notice that the Pinus virginiana *'Wate's Golden' (1) is now screaming yellow,* Cryptomeria japonica *'Elegans' (3) has turned to a wonderful smoky plum color, and the blue of* Chamaecyparis lawsoniana *'Pelt's Blue' (2) is more intense this time of year.*

In the midstory the contorted filbert Corylus avellana *'Contorta' (B) has catkins and that wonderful winter bark is in evidence.* Thuja orientalis *'Sunlight' (3) has burnished gold on the tips. There are flowers on* Mahonia ×media *'Charity' (E).* Pinus contorta *var.* latifolia *'Chief Joseph' (7), which was not even noticed in the summer, is now a high-pitched yellow.* Abies procera *(Glauca Group) 'Nana' (11) has taken on a more powdery blue hue.* Chamaecyparis lawsoniana *'Duncanii' (5) has stayed tight; it didn't splay out with the snow two weeks earlier. The same is true for* Pinus aristata *'Sherwood*

Compact' (10) and Juniperus communis *'Compressa' (1).* Hamamelis ×intermedia *'Primavera' and 'Diane' (C) will soon burst into flower.*

In the understory the heather, Calluna vulgaris *'Aurea' (1) that was gold in the summer is now green. The sedge,* Carex comans *bronze-leaved (3), looks fantastic, doesn't it? And the grass* Pennisetum alopecuroides *'Little Bunny' (4) has its tawny winter color.* Calluna vulgaris *'Mousehole' (9) has turned a fantastic smoky plum color and the* Sedum rupestre *'Angelina' (11) is a nice orangish color.*

Entrance to the garden in winter. *Thuja orientalis* 'Sunlight' is a little exclamation point and anchors the island but doesn't obscure the view. The blue of *Picea pungens* 'Glauca Globosa' is repeated on both sides of the curved path and is echoed further back with *P. pungens* 'Fat Albert'. Although bigger, taller, and more upright, 'Fat Albert' makes the space look less narrow. In another "optical confusion," the tall blue spruce to the left, *P. pungens* 'Thompsonii', blocks the view of a utility pole across the street. On the right in front of the porch is *Chamaecyparis obtusa* 'Gold Fern', bumped out from the foundation to make a sinewy path to the front steps. A space-filler most of the year, *Cornus sanguinea* 'Midwinter Fire' is a knockout in winter, distracting viewers from the road behind it.

Another view of the front garden in winter. The smoky plum color of *Cryptomeria japonica* 'Elegans' and a gold scrub pine (*Pinus virginiana* 'Wate's Golden') pulls the viewer into the garden. To the far left, the exposed stems of *Betula pendula* 'Youngii' are both elegant and simple, and their plumy brown color matches the nearby daphne and *Berberis* 'Concorde'. The bright blue pot brings the eye down and makes the space more intimate, like a wooded area. In the foreground is *Chamaecyparis obtusa* 'Gold Fern'.

CASSANDRA'S FAVORITE PLANTS FOR
CAMEO SPOTS IN THE MIXED BORDER WITH CONIFERS

◆ Acer palmatum *'Sango-kaku': Wonderful foliage in season, nice fall color, and great coral stems in the winter against a dark green backdrop. I also like the Japanese maples with variegated foliage. Oh, and don't forget A. pensylvanicum 'Erythrocladum' with its yummy cardinal red stems.*

◆ Betula pendula *'Youngii': A favorite choice. This weeping birch is deciduous with yellow fall color but not messy, and in winter the stems are smoky plum-colored. When they are wet with rain or foggy mists, the stems hold beads of water glistening like little drops of crystal. This does not take much space in the border but makes the bed appear wider. I call it "optical confusion."*

◆ Cercis canadensis *'Forest Pansy': Great for an accent in a bed. I really like it but it does not do well for us and is short-lived.*

◆ Cornus alternifolia *'Argentea': Smaller than C. controversa 'Variegata'. I love the bark and the tiered branching habit.*

◆ Sambucus nigra *'Pulverulenta': For a border on the north side. In addition to beautiful white and pink variegated foliage, it has lacy pink flowers and produces much fruit for the birds. It's a great mid-sized plant that can fit in a narrow border. Other elderberries include S. nigra 'Black Beauty' and 'Black Lace', and S. racemosa 'Sutherland Gold' and 'Goldenlocks'.*

◆ Styrax japonica *'Carillon': Small to mid-size with a dramatic but narrow weeping habit. It has small fragrant white bell-shaped flowers. Styrax japonica 'Emerald Pagoda' is even smaller with the same weeping habit.*

Appendix

Coping with Deer

IN RECENT TIMES, damage to ornamental plants caused by white-tailed deer (*Odocoileus virginianus*) has become an increasingly widespread problem in some parts of the United States. Once only a rural annoyance, it is now a complaint of suburban gardeners.

A number of circumstances have contributed to the problem. The large predators of deer have disappeared because of the clear-cutting for agriculture which at the same time has created browsing habitat for deer. The deer population is continually losing more of its accustomed haunts with residential subdivisions cropping up everywhere.

To keep deer out of the garden, it has been suggested to place various repellents throughout the garden, including bags of hair, fragrant soaps, various herbal and garlic preparations, and countless widely marketed commercial concoctions. These methods are usually effective only if the deer pressure is light, and, even then, most work only temporarily.

The only dependable remedy is to exclude the deer with tall fences, an expensive and often unsightly solution. Smaller specimen plants

Erecting a plastic mesh barrier may be necessary to protect a valued specimen.

A well-constructed permanent deer fence.

can be protected with chicken wire cages. Dogs, especially beagles, are often effective provided they are in the garden at night.

Another strategy is planning your garden space by placing susceptible plants only in protected areas, perhaps close to the house or in a fenced yard, or in a ring of less-preferred species or barrier plants.

A deer will eat between 6 and 7 pounds (2.7 and 4.5 kg) of vegetation a day. Whether a deer targets a particular plant species depends on many factors besides palatability: weather conditions, availability of preferred foods, seasonal factors, snow cover, and movement patterns all play a part.

Damage by deer is often most apparent in early spring when the young tender foliage is emerging from buds. A plant considered resistant in one part of the country can be ravaged in another. It is advisable to consult plant preference lists generated in the gardener's own locale.

Unfortunately, the damage to conifers is often irreversible if the foliage is chewed to bare wood. Landscaping with deer-resistant species is a more aesthetically satisfying alternative.

DEER CANDY

- *Taxus* (yew): Fortunately, it sprouts from bare wood.
- *Thuja occidentalis* (eastern arborvitae): Unfortunately, it does not sprout from bare wood.

CONIFERS ALMOST NEVER BROWSED BY DEER

- *Cephalotaxus* (plum-yew)
- *Chamaecyparis pisifera* (sawara-cypress)
- *Cunninghamia lanceolata* (China-fir)
- *Juniperus* ssp. (juniper)
- *Microbiota decussata* (Siberian cypress)
- *Picea*, except *P. orientalis* (spruce, except oriental spruce)
- *Pinus* (pine)
- *Pseudotsuga menziesii* (Douglas-fir)

CONIFERS SELDOM BROWSED BY DEER

- *Abies* (fir)
- *Cedrus* (cedar)
- *Chamaecyparis nootkatensis* (Alaska-cedar)
- *Chamaecyparis obtusa* (hinoki false cypress)
- *Chamaecyparis thyoides* (Atlantic white-cedar)
- *Cryptomeria japonica* (Japanese-cedar)
- ×*Cupressocyparis leylandii* (Leyland cypress)
- *Thuja plicata* (giant arborvitae)
- *Tsuga* (hemlock)

Conifers for Wet Spots

These conifers tolerate very wet conditions, even standing water part of the year.

Chamaecyparis thyoides (Atlantic white-cedar, swamp-cedar)

A tree of freshwater swamps in its native habitat, swamp-cedar grows in full sun to 30 to 50 ft. (9 to 15 m) tall. It is an important timber tree because of the durability of its wood in contact with the soil, although it is not widely used as a garden plant. 'Ericoides' is an oval, compact shrub with soft gray-green foliage that turns a deep violet-brown in winter. 'Heatherbun' is a dwarf globe with soft, fuzzy, medium green foliage turning a hazy heather-purple in winter; it reaches 6 to 8 ft. (1.8 to 2.5 m) tall and contrasts nicely with other conifers.

Larix laricina (American larch)

A tolerant, wide-ranging species native to cold regions, American larch will survive in conditions that are far too wet for most woody plants. 'Blue Sparkler' is a vigorous grower with excellent blue foliage; it reaches 5 ft. (1.5 m) tall. 'Craftsbury Flats' is a dwarf round ball of pale green foliage; it matures at 4 ft. (1.2 m) tall.

Metasequoia glyptostroboides (dawn redwood).

Dawn redwood is very tolerant of wet, even boggy soil for part of the year. It rapidly reaches 40 to 50 ft. (12 to 15 m) tall in fewer than 20 years. The foliage is deciduous (see photo).

Taxodium distichum (bald-cypress).

Bald-cypress is very tolerant of wet conditions. It reaches 50 ft. (15 m) tall in cultivation and is very long-lived. Like dawn redwood, it has deciduous foliage (see photo).

CONIFERS FOR SOUTHERN GARDENS

SOUTHERN SUMMERS in the United States are long and hot, and many species of conifers suffer in that climate. Fortunately, several succeed in heat. In addition to the species described in detail here, several others have been covered in other sections of this book:

Calocedrus decurrens (incense-cedar)
Cryptomeria japonica (Japanese-cedar)
Cunninghamia lanceolata (China-fir)
Cupressus arizonica (Arizona cypress)
×*Cupressocyparis leylandii* (Leyland cypress)
Metasequoia glyptostroboides (dawn redwood)

Araucaria araucana (monkey-puzzle tree)

The monkey-puzzle tree is a native of Chile and has grown in the Southern Hemisphere for millions of years. It always has a single very straight stem with the branches whorled around it. It is slow-growing in youth but with age becomes dome-shaped above a bare trunk (see photo).

CONIFERS FOR SUMMER-DRY AREAS

- *Calocedrus decurrens* (incense-cedar)
- *Cedrus atlantica* (Atlas cedar)
- *Cedrus deodara* (deodar cedar)
- *Cupressus arizonica* (Arizona cypress)
- *Cupressus sempervirens* (Italian cypress)
- *Ginkgo biloba* (maidenhair tree)
- *Juniperus* (juniper)
- *Pinus* (pine)

Cedrus deodara (deodar cedar)

The true cedars adapt to a wide range of soils and are famously toler-ant of hot, dry situations. There are four species, all mainly suitable for large gardens or public landscapes. Since cedars are rather spindly in youth, they are often planted too close to structures. Given space and time, they are magnificent in maturity. Many selections of deodar cedar will grow in southern gardens.

'Aurea' (golden deodar cedar): fast-growing, golden-yellow needles in spring turn yellow-green, best color in full sun.

'Cream Puff': a shrub with white-tipped young foliage, reaches 1 ft. (0.3 m) tall by 3 ft. (0.9 m) wide in 10 years.

'Crystal Falls': soft blue foliage, elegant pendulous habit, fine-tex-tured, reaches 30 ft. (9 m) tall and wide.

'Devinely Blue': a wide-spreading, flat-topped mound with pale gray-green new growth, drooping branch tips (see photo).

'Feelin Blue': a dwarf spreading form with gray-blue foliage, reach-es 1 ft. (0.3 m) tall by 3 ft. (0.9 m) wide in 10 years (see photo).

'Golden Horizon': semi-prostrate and flat-topped with gracefully weeping branches, spreads 2 to 4 ft. (0.6 to 1.2 m), golden foliage in full sun.

'Karl Fuchs': very blue foliage, for the larger landscape (see photo).

'Kashmir': foliage silver blue-green, also for the larger landscape.

'Pygmy': an extremely slow-growing dwarf, less than $\frac{2}{3}$ in. (1.7 cm) a year, useful for trough garden, blue-green needles $\frac{1}{2}$ in. (1.2 cm) long.

'Roman Gold': broad irregular cone, dense bright golden-yellow fo-liage (see photo).

'Sander's Blue': one of the bluest weepers, reaches 50 ft. (15 m) tall by 30 ft. (9 m) wide.

'Shalimar': soft blue foliage, graceful habit, upright tree form.

Cedrus libani (cedar of Lebanon)

Atlas cedar (*Cedrus atlantica*, probably a subspecies of *C. libani*) is widely grown in more northerly areas, but two selections of cedar of Lebanon are also suitable for southern gardens.

'Aurea': slow-growing to 50 ft. (15 m) tall, pyramidal form, needles golden yellow with green base, best color in winter.

'Green Prince': slow-growing, 1 in. (2.5 cm) a year, a deep green dwarf that becomes an open-branched pyramid giving the appear-ance of great age, excellent for trough gardens or bonsai.

Juniperus virginiana (eastern red-cedar)

The most widespread of all the native conifers in eastern North America, *Juniperus virginiana* is found from Nova Scotia to northern Florida and west to the Dakotas and Texas. No conifer is tougher or less finicky, though it does best in full sun with good drainage. It tolerates drought, heat, and cold, and difficult site situations. A few of the dozens of cultivars are described here.

'Burkii': columnar with a straight stem and ascending branches, dense blue-green foliage, bronzes in winter.

'Canaertii': upright, eventually opens up, dense dark green foliage all seasons, abundant blue cones.

'Corcorcor': narrow and conical, remains a rich green all seasons, rapid growing, sturdy and dependable, reaches 25 to 30 ft. (8 to 9 m) tall, also called 'Emerald Sentinel' (see photo).

'Grey Owl': soft dusty silver-gray foliage and abundant silver-gray cones, grows slowly into a wide-spreading shrub 3 ft. (0.9 m) tall by 6 ft. 1.8 m) wide (see photo). Exceptional.

'Silver Spreader': low groundcovering shrub, bright silver-gray in summer, more gray-green in winter, thick and coarse foliage, undemanding.

Taxodium distichum (bald-cypress)

Another North American native conifer that is found in swamps from Delaware south to Florida is the deciduous bald-cypress (see photo).

Taxodium distichum
'Secrest'

It reaches 50 ft. (15 m) tall in cultivation and is very long-lived. Tough and adaptable, bald-cypress will survive standing in water for half of the growing season but is also tolerant of dry soil. The feathery foliage turns russet or a soft brown in fall. Several selections are worth mentioning.

'Cascade Falls': a pendulous large shrub or small tree, not exceeding 20 ft. (6 m) tall, with sage-green foliage and red-brown bark (see photo).

'Mickelson': upright branching, narrowly pyramidal, fast-growing, adaptable for urban conditions, orange-bronze fall color, reaches 75 ft. (23 m) tall by 20 ft. (6 m) wide, also called 'Shawnee Brave'.

'Peve Minaret': spire-shaped, reaching 12 ft. (3.6 m) tall by 3 ft. (0.9 m) wide in 10 years, fine-textured overlapping needles, bright green in summer turning rusty red in fall.

'Secrest': globose, flat-topped, grows 3 to 6 in. (7.5 to 15 cm) a year to 6 ft. (1.8 m) tall.

Taxus (yew)

Yews (described elsewhere in this book) do well except in the southernmost areas, where plum-yew (*Cephalotaxus*, also described elsewhere) is a good substitute. Plum-yews tolerate shade. 'Prostrata' is low-growing and requires less pruning to maintain it (see photo). 'Fastigiata' could be used for hedging (see photo).

CONIFERS AS CHRISTMAS TREES

WHAT MAKES A GOOD HOLIDAY TREE?

- Needles: rich dark green or blue-green in color, remaining on the tree for a long time after it is cut, relatively soft, and easy to handle, with a pleasant fragrance and free from pungent odors.

- Branches: capable of supporting ornaments but not so thick that it is difficult to hang them, sufficiently durable to tolerate shipment.

- Habit: conical form, with sufficient foliage and branch density to appear full crowned.

- Growth rate: sufficiently rapid to produce an attractive tree of saleable size in 7 to 10 years.

Abies (fir)

Fragrance, color, and good needle retention after being cut make firs favorite trees both in Europe and North America. Balsam fir (*Abies balsamea*) is one of the most popular. Native over a large area of eastern Canada and northeastern United States, it has a pleasant fragrance and deep green needles, and when cut retains its needles even in warm, dry rooms. It has a symmetrical shape and stiff boughs capable of holding ornaments. At one time pillows were commonly stuffed with its soft and fragrant needles.

Fraser fir (*Abies fraseri*), which grows in the southern United States, is also a favorite. It holds its soft needles longer than any other tree. Concolor fir (*A. concolor*) is popular in the southwestern United States despite its relatively slow growth rate (see photo). Other firs are grand fir (*A. grandis*) and noble fir (*A. procera*), the latter considered the premier holiday tree. Native to the northwestern United States and Canada, noble fir is best for holding large ornaments. Interestingly, in Germany and Denmark the principal species grown for the holiday is Nordmann fir (*A. nordmanniana*), which in the United States is valued as a choice specimen tree for the landscape.

Juniperus virginiana (eastern red-cedar)

Eastern red-cedar is occasionally used in the southern United States, but in northerly areas it takes on a purplish cast during the winter.

Picea (spruce)

The spruces are considered traditional CHRISTMAS trees especially in Europe but they have very poor needle retention and the foliage often has unpleasant pungent odors. Norway spruce (*Picea abies*) was one of the first trees to be used as a Christmas tree in Europe and its dark needles make it a popular choice. White spruce (*P. glauca*) has nice gray-green foliage color and habit, but the needles stink when crushed and the tree is slow-growing. Colorado spruce (*P. pungens*) has excellent blue-green needle color and good form but very sharp needles which make it difficult to decorate.

Pinus (pine)

Many species are popular and they are easy to grow on plantations because of their fast growth rate. Scots pine (*Pinus sylvestris*) is extremely well-liked. It responds well to shearing, which results in a tree with a dense conical crown, and also it can be grown in cold climates. Eastern white pine (*P. strobus*) is highly favored, in part, because the needles stay on for a long time after cutting. This pine has a rapid growth rate but must be sheared to ensure good form and foliage density. Of course, its branches are brittle which means it does not lend itself well to long-distance shipping.

Pseudotsuga menziesii (Douglas-fir)

Popular in western North America, where it is native, Douglas-fir has all the qualities desired in a Christmas tree, except that is grows slowly and requires more than 10 years to produce a saleable tree (see photo).

German Grave Plantings

In Germany, designing and maintaining gravesites is considered a way of doing something for the late person or giving something back to the person who passed away. It is a way to show respect and gratitude for the dead person. Quite the opposite is the case in the United States, where grave sites are usually visited only during special holidays or anniversaries and cut flowers rather than living plants are usually placed by the memorial stones.

Germans view cemeteries as places for the living as well as the dead. A grave site is not only the final resting place of a relative or friend, but a place to remember the person and have a dialog with them. The design is supposed to reflect memories of the person and their personality and character. The gravesite expresses how much the departed person is valued, appreciated, and respected by those close to him.

Families in Germany often visit cemeteries just to enjoy the nature. They go for a walk in the cemetery just like in a city park, even if they don't have a grave there to visit.

Gravesites in northern Germany.

Certified professional cemetery gardeners help with the plant selection, design, and long-term maintenance of grave sites. The stonemasons are specialists also and the meaning of the grave site and its design is applied to the tombstone itself. In addition to their ornamental and cultural characteristics, most genera of conifers and many herbaceous plants carry traditional symbolism which will influence the plant choices in a design.

Conifers are usually the tallest plants and are often paced at the side of the stone. They frame the grave and ensure the three-dimensional appearance of the grave site. They are the important permanent plantings and provide an attractive appearance all year. Slow-growing cultivars are selected and the gardeners will need to do corrective pruning to maintain shape and size. Low-growing conifers can be used as the groundcovering part of the grave. The groundcovers are used to prevent the growth of weeds and prevent the soil from drying out. Conifer branches are also used in the winter season to cover up the grave to protect it from frosts.

Juniperus squamata 'Blue Star' and *Euonymus fortunei* 'Emerald Gaiety' in a German gravesite planting.

PLACES TO SEE CONIFERS

Arboretum Trompenburg, Rotterdam, Netherlands
Atlanta Botanical Garden, Atlanta, Georgia
Bedgebury National Pinetum, Surrey, England
Berlin Botanic Garden, Germany
Bickelhaupt Arboretum, Clinton, Iowa
Bressingham Gardens, Norfolk, England
Chanticleer Gardens, Wayne, Pennsylvania
Chicago Botanic Garden, Glencoe, Illinois
Cleveland Botanical Garden, Cleveland, Ohio
The Dawes Arboretum, Newark, Ohio
Denver Botanic Gardens, Denver, Colorado
Hidden Lake Gardens, Tipton, Michigan
JC Raulston Arboretum, Raleigh, North Carolina
Montreal Botanical Garden, Québec, Canada
Missouri Botanical Garden, St. Louis, Missouri
Morton Arboretum, Lisle, Illinois
Munich Botanic Garden, Germany
New Botanical Garden, Hamburg, Germany
The Oregon Garden, Silverton, Oregon
Planten un Blomen, Hamburg, Germany
Royal Botanic Garden, Edinburgh, Scotland
Royal Botanic Gardens, Kew, England
Royal Horticulture Society Garden, Wisley, England
San Francisco Botanical Garden at Strybing Arboretum, California
Scott Arboretum of Swarthmore College, Swarthmore, Pennsylvania
VanDusen Botanical Garden, Vancouver, British Columbia, Canada
University of Wisconsin Arboretum, Madison, Wisconsin
U.S. National Arboretum, Washington, DC

For additional listings in the United States, go to the website
of the American Association of Botanical Gardens and Arboreta,
www.aabga.org.

PLACES TO SEE
BONSAI COLLECTIONS

Belgium Bonsai Museum, Ginkgo Bonsai Centre, Lochristi, Belgium

Birmingham Botanical Gardens, England (home of the National Bonsai Collection)

Bonsai Centrum Heidelberg-Wieblingen, Germany

Bonsaiville, Auckland, New Zealand

Brisbane Botanic Gardens, Queensland, Australia

Montreal Botanical Garden, Québec, Canada

Pacific Rim Bonsai Collection, Federal Way, Washington

Royal Horticultural Society Garden at Wisley, Surrey, England

U.S. National Arboretum, Washington, DC (home of the National Bonsai Collection)

INDEX

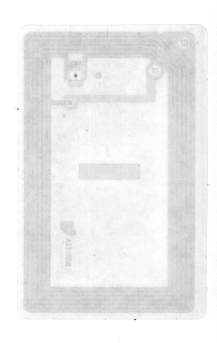